UNIDIR
United Nations Institute for Disarm
Geneva

Disarmament and Conflict Resolution Project

Managing Arms in Peace Processes: Aspects of Psychological and Intelligence

Paper: *Andrei Raevsky*

Project funded by: the Ford Foundation, the United States Institute of Peace, the Winston Foundation, the Ploughshares Fund, the John D. and Catherine T. MacArthur Foundation; and the governments of Argentina, Austria, Brazil, Finland, France, Germany, Malta, the Netherlands, Norway, South Africa, Sweden, the United Kingdom, and the United States of America.

NOTE

The designations employed and the presentation of the material in this publication do not imply the expression of any opinion whatsoever on the part of the Secretariat of the United Nations concerning the legal status of any country, territory, city or area, or of its authorities, or concerning the delimitation of its frontiers or boundaries.

*

* *

The views expressed in this paper are those of the authors and do not necessarily reflect the views of the United Nations Secretariat.

UNIDIR/96/31

UNITED NATIONS PUBLICATION

Sales No. GV.E.96.0.21

ISBN 92-9045-116-5

Table of Contents

Previous DCR Project Publications

Managing Arms in Peace Processes: Somalia

Managing Arms in Peace Processes: Rhodesia/Zimbabwe

Managing Arms in Peace Processes: Croatia and Bosnia-Herzegovina

Managing Arms in Peace Processes: Cambodia

Managing Arms in Peace Processes: Mozambique

Small Arms Management and Peacekeeping in Southern Africa

Managing Arms in Peace Processes: Liberia

Preface

Under the heading of Collective Security, UNIDIR is conducting a major project on Disarmament and Conflict Resolution (DCR). The project examines the utility and modalities of disarming warring parties as an element of efforts to resolve intra-state conflicts. It collects field experiences regarding the demobilization and disarmament of warring factions; reviews 11 collective security actions where disarmament has been attempted; and examines the role that disarmament of belligerents can play in the management and resolution of internal conflicts. The 11 cases are UNPROFOR (Yugoslavia), UNOSOM and UNITAF (Somalia), UNAVEM (Angola), UNTAC (Cambodia), ONUSAL (El Salvador), ONUCA (Central America), UNTAG (Namibia), ONUMOZ (Mozambique), UNOMIL (Liberia), UNMIH (Haiti), and the 1979 Commonwealth operation in Rhodesia. In addition to the case studies, there will be four volumes of papers that independently address certain issues that emerged from the case studies. The issue papers deal with training in peacekeeping, small arms and peacekeeping in Southern Africa, broader issues that are critically important for the success or failure of disarmament and conflict resolution, and finally, psychological operations and intelligence. The last of which pertains to this particular volume.

Being an autonomous institute charged with the task of undertaking independent, applied research, UNIDIR keeps a certain distance from political actors of all kinds. The impact of our publications is predicated on the independence with which we are seen to conduct our research. At the same time, being a research institute within the framework of the United Nations, UNIDIR naturally relates its work to the needs of the Organization. Inspired by the Secretary-General's report on "New Dimensions of Arms Regulation and Disarmament in the Post-Cold War Era",[1] the DCR Project also relates to a great many governments involved in peace operations through the UN or under regional auspices. Last but not least, comprehensive networks of communication and cooperation have been developed with UN personnel having field experience.

Weapons-wise, the disarmament of warring parties is mostly a matter of light weapons. These weapons account for as much as 90% of the casualties in many armed conflicts. UNIDIR recently published a paper on this subject (*Small Arms and Intra-State Conflicts*, UNIDIR Paper No. 34, 1995). The Secretary-General's

---

[1] Document A/C.1/47/7, No. 31, 23 October 1992.

appeal for stronger efforts to control small arms - to promote "micro disarmament"[2] - is one which UNIDIR will continue to attend to in the framework of the DCR Project.

This report focuses upon particular aspects of peace operations, namely, psychological operations (PSYOPs) and intelligence activities. Although much has been written about peace operations, psychological operations and intelligence have been largely ignored. This report addresses the importance of PSYOPs and intelligence activities as an essential component of peace operations. Mr. Raevsky, who served as a researcher on the DCR Project emphasizes that the local population should be informed about the aims of the peacekeeping force; that intelligence is an inherent part of any military operation, peace operations included; and that the skillful use of intelligence and PSYOPs for the preparation and execution of peace operations reduces the risk of "mission creep".

I would like to thank the staff at UNIDIR who assisted in the publication process: Virginia Gamba, for leading the DCR project until the end of March 1996; our Editor, Lara Bernini, and two Interns, Mike MacKinnon and Alessandra Fabrello, for editing this volume; and our Specialized Publications Secretary, Anita Blétry, for designing and producing the camera-ready copy.

UNIDIR takes no position on the views or conclusions expressed in this report. They are Mr. Raevsky's. I am grateful to him for his contribution: UNIDIR has been happy to have such a resourceful and dedicated collaborator.

Sverre Lodgaard
Director, UNIDIR

---

[2] Document 50/60-S/1995/1, 3 January 1995.

Acknowledgements

The DCR Project takes this opportunity to thank the many foundations and governments who have contributed financially and with personnel to the establishment and evolution of the research associated with the Project. Among our contributors, the following deserve a special mention and our deep appreciation: the Ford Foundation, the United States Institute of Peace, the Winston Foundation, the Ploughshares Fund, the John D. and Catherine T. MacArthur Foundation, and the governments of Argentina, Austria, Brazil, Finland, France, Germany, Malta, the Netherlands, Norway, Sweden, South Africa, the United Kingdom, and the United States of America.

Project Introduction

Disarmament and Conflict Resolution

The global arena's main preoccupation during the Cold War centred on the maintenance of international peace and stability between states. The vast network of alliances, obligations and agreements which bound nuclear superpowers to the global system, and the memory of the rapid internationalization of disputes into world wars, favored the formulation of national and multinational deterrent policies designed to maintain a stability which was often confused with immobility. In these circumstances, the ability of groups within states to engage in protest and to challenge recognized authority was limited.

The end of the Cold War in 1989, however, led to a relaxing of this pattern, generating profound mobility within the global system. The ensuing break-up of alliances, partnerships, and regional support systems brought new and often weak states into the international arena. Since weak states are susceptible to ethnic tensions, secession, and outright criminality, many regions are now afflicted by situations of violent intra-state conflict.

Intra-state conflict occurs at immense humanitarian cost. The massive movement of people, their desperate condition, and the direct and indirect tolls on human life have, in turn, generated pressure for international action, most notably from the UN.

The reputation of the United Nations as being representative of all states and thus as being objective and trustworthy has been especially valued, as indicated by the greater number of peace operations in which it is currently engaged. Before 1991, the UN peace operations' presence enhanced not only peace but also the strengthening of democratic processes, conciliation among population groups, the encouragement of respect for human rights, and the alleviation of humanitarian problems. These achievements are exemplified by the role of the UN in Congo, southern Lebanon, Nicaragua, Namibia, El Salvador, and to a lesser extent in Haiti.

Nevertheless, since 1991 the United Nations has been engaged in a number of simultaneous, larger, and more ambitious peace operations in Africa, such as those in Angola, Cambodia, Somalia, Mozambique, and the former Yugoslavia. It has been increasingly pressured to act on quick-flaring and horrendously costly explosions of violence such as that in Rwanda. The financial, personnel, and timing pressure on the United Nations to undertake these massive short-term stabilizing actions has seriously impaired the UN's ability to ensure long-term national and regional stability. The UN has necessarily shifted its focus from a supporting role, in which it could ensure long-term national and international stability, to a role which involves obtaining quick peace and easing humanitarian pressures immediately. But without a focus on peace defined in terms of longer-term stability, the overall success of efforts to mediate and resolve intra-state conflict will remain in question.

This problem has gained some recognition and resulted in belated action by the international community. More and more organizations and governments are linking success to the ability to offer non-violent alternatives to a post-conflict society. These alternatives are mostly of a socio-political/economic nature, and are national rather than regional in character. As important as these linkages are to the final resolution of conflict, they tend to overlook a major source of instability: the existence of vast amounts of weapons widely distributed among combatant and non-combatant elements in societies which are emerging from long periods of internal conflict.

The reason why weapons themselves are not the primary focus of attention in the reconstruction of post-conflict societies is because they are viewed from a political perspective. Action which does not award importance to disarmament processes is justified by invoking the political value of a weapon as well as the way the weapon is used by a warring party, rather than its mere existence and availability. Proponents of this action argue that peace takes away the reason for using the weapon and, therefore, renders it harmless for the post-conflict reconstruction process. And yet, easy availability of weapons can, and does, militarize societies in general. It also destabilizes regions that are affected by unrestricted trade of light weapons between borders.

There are two problems with the international community's approach to post-conflict reconstruction processes: on the one hand, the international community, under pressure to react to increasingly violent internal conflict, has put a higher value on peace in the short-term than on development and stability in the long-term; and, on the other hand, those who *do* focus on long-term stability have put a higher value on the social and economic elements of development than on the management of the primary tools of violence, i.e., weapons and munitions.

Given these considerations, the DCR Project believes that the way to implement peace, defined in terms of long-term stability, is to focus not just on the sources of violence (such as social and political development issues) but also on the material vehicles for violence (such as weapons and munitions). Likewise, the implementation of peace must take into account *both* the future needs of a society and the elimination of its excess weapons, *and also* the broader international and regional context in which the society is situated. This is because weapons that are not managed and controlled in the field will invariably flow over into neighboring countries, becoming a problem in themselves. Thus, *the establishment of viable stability requires that three primary aspects be included in every approach to intra-state conflict resolution: (1) the implementation of a comprehensive, systematic disarmament program as soon as a peace operation is set-up; (2) the establishment of an arms management program that continues into national post-conflict reconstruction processes; and (3) the encouragement of close cooperation on weapons control and management programs between countries in the region where the peace operation is being implemented.*

In order to fulfill its research mission, the DCR Project has been divided into four phases. These are as follows: (1) the development, distribution, and interpretation of a *Practitioners' Questionnaire on Weapons Control, Disarmament and Demobilization during Peacekeeping Operations*; (2) the development and publication of case studies on peace operations in which disarmament tasks constituted an important aspect of the wider mission; (3) the organization of a series of workshops on policy issues; and (4) the publication of policy papers on substantive issues related to the linkages between the management of arms during peace processes (MAPP) and the settlement of conflict.

Between September 1995 and May 1996, the Project foresees four sets of publications. The first of these will involve eleven case studies, covering peace operations in Somalia, Rhodesia/Zimbabwe, Bosnia/Croatia, Central America (ONUCA and ONUSAL), Cambodia, Angola, Namibia, Mozambique, Liberia and Haiti. The second set of publications will involve one volume of three papers on the relationship between arms and conflict in the region of Southern Africa. The third set of publications will include nine policy papers, addressing topics such as Security Council Procedures, Mandate Specificity, Doctrine, Rules of Engagement, Coercive versus Consensual Arms Control and Demobilization Processes, Consensus, Intelligence and Media, and Training. These policy papers will appear in three different volumes, as follows: ***Disarmament Training for Peacekeepers: A Status Report; Managing Arms during Peace Processes: Information Gathering for Disarmament Operations; and The Management of Arms during Peace Processes: Disarmament and Peace.***

In order to manage arms during peace missions, military commanders need to be able to detect the movement of belligerent forces, determine the location of hidden arms cashes, and anticipate the plans and tactics of those who intend to violate agreements and threaten the execution of the mission mandate. This boils down to a need for a sound information gathering, assessment and distribution system in the theater of operations. Nearly all respondents to the UNIDIR questionnaire, for example, mention the need for a proper intelligence system during peace operations. The importance of this capability cannot be over emphasized. Related to good intelligence is the need to be a step ahead of the opposition and to anticipate their moves. When confronted with periodic violations, deliberate breaches of agreements and even sporadic attacks, it is important to have information to anticipate and prepare in a preemptive manner to counter or lessen the effect thereof on the overall success of the mission. Accurate warning will allow more effective counter measures and provide an opportunity to disrupt threatening behavior before it is launched. This requires good intelligence, the ability to evaluate and disseminate information, and the ability to react rapidly.

Despite the importance of this element in many aspects of the successful implementation of a peace operation, information gathering in the field (even though it relates to the enforcement of consensual disarmament) has been neglected, at best, or shunned, at worst. To address this problem the Project has undertaken a study on information gathering and peacekeeping, presented in this volume by Andrei Raevsky.

Virginia Gamba
Project Director
Geneva, March 1996

Definitions

For the purposes of this paper, a number of concepts have been used with a meaning which does not necessarily correspond to their use in other contexts:

- ***Peacekeeping***: the term "peacekeeping" includes all Chapter VI and the so-called "Chapter VI and a half" operations (with enforcement aspects), but not operations designed from the outset as Chapter VII operations.

- ***Psychological Operations (PSYOPs)***: used here to mean "efforts aimed at inducing or reinforcing attitudes favorable to the (peacekeeping) operation in the population of the host country". Sometimes also referred to as "public information". This definition is a transposition of the US concept of Psychological Operations (PSYOPs) to a peacekeeping mission. As used here, PSYOPs are designed as local efforts limited to the mission area.

- ***Intelligence***: activities aimed at collecting, analyzing and disseminating information among the peacekeeping force and within the national authorities which have dispatched it to the mission area or formulated its mandate. While the scope of such activities can range from tactical battlefield intelligence to strategic intelligence, in the context of a peacekeeping mission it is usually limited to the area of intelligence responsibility: this includes the mission area and the areas adjacent to it which can influence the mission area.

- ***Civil Affairs (CA)***: activities that establish, maintain, influence, or exploit relations between military forces, civil authorities (both governmental and non-governmental), and the civilian populace in a friendly, neutral, or hostile area, before, during, after or in lieu of other military operations. Civil affairs may include the performance by military forces or UN civil organizations of activities and functions that are normally the responsibility of local governments.

- ***Force Multipliers***: capabilities which boost the overall effectiveness and optimal allocation of resources of a force or part of a force.

- ***Mission Creep***: occurs when the original scope and aims of a mission are gradually expanding or changing in nature and in a manner clearly not foreseen when the mission was planned.

- ***Mandate Creep***: successive redefinitions of a mandate in reaction to a changing situation in the field (this usually implies an expansion of the mandate and/or an escalation in the use, or threat of use, of force); mandate creep is a political reaction to a situation of mission creep.

I. Introduction

> He who wins the intelligence and PSYOP battles may not have to wage a subsequent combat arms battle (or may wage it at lower intensity) and will have a far greater chance of operational and strategic victory than his adversary.
>
> Major William H. Burgess III[1]

While much has been recently written about peacekeeping operations, two of their aspects have been largely overlooked: information/psychological operations and intelligence. Information/psychological operations deal with the deliberate dissemination of information to the public in any country including the one hosting the peacekeeping operation with the aim of obtaining support and acceptance of the peacekeeping force and its mission. Intelligence consists of the collection, analysis and delivery of information to officials within the peacekeeping force and to the authorities mandating the force (United Nations, regional, or other) for the purpose of assisting the decision-making processes and policy formulations. Although information and intelligence are crucial for the success of any military operation, they have been largely ignored for peacekeeping operations and official UN documents carefully avoid this subject.

The reasons for this reticence to discuss issues of information and intelligence are numerous. Intelligence activities, and particularly intelligence gathering, are often perceived as hostile, almost aggressive, activities; as something "improper" which decent "soldiers of peace" would not do. As for information activities, they are all too often perceived as being either the job of the mass-media or the activity of manipulative governments or interest groups. These are dangerous misconceptions. Simply put, intelligence constitutes the "eyes", the "ears" and part of the "brain" of any military force; without a solid and well-adapted intelligence capability any military force becomes blind, deaf and disoriented. As for information capabilities, they represent the "voice" of the force, which can enable the force to "talk rather than shoot"; in this sense, information is a crucial asset for any force trying to minimize combat and casualties.

---

[1] Major William H. Burgess III, "Towards a More Complete Doctrine - SOF in Air and Battle Future", *Military Review*, February 1991, p. 36.

The peacekeeping operations in the former Yugoslavia and Somalia have shown that peacekeeping operations can be very difficult and dangerous. This is particularly true for the so-called "chapter six and a half" operations which are in the grey zone between peacekeeping and peacemaking. Because such operations imply a limited and carefully-directed use of force, intelligence is crucial for discrimination and targeting purposes, while information is important for the explanation of the reasons which justify the use of force. Failure to carefully and skillfully use intelligence and psychological operations (PSYOPs) in the course of the preparation and execution of any peacekeeping operation, but particularly in a "chapter six and a half" -type of operation, yields a great risk of so-called "mission creep" (i.e., escalation, mandate enlargement, increase in the commitment of forces and means, etc.).

All peacekeeping operations are primarily *political* in nature. Hence, their success or failure is essentially a result of political factors, or perceptions. Furthermore, the general public of the states hosting peacekeeping operations do not, usually, have a clear understanding of the task, mission, scope, mandate, etc. of the peacekeeping force. This often leads to disillusionment, mistrust, suspicion or even outright hostility towards the peacekeeping forces. The examples of Somalia and Yugoslavia have shown that the population of the host country cannot be ignored in the planning and execution of a mission. This is not only a matter of "doing the right thing", but also a matter of "explaining what is being aimed at". Simply put, *unless the local population knows the aims of the peacekeeping force, tensions will arise no matter how well intentioned the peacekeepers are*. Furthermore, Somalia and Yugoslavia have also clearly shown that a lack of understanding of the local culture can lead a peacekeeping mission into an impasse: *no amount of threats or force will ever be an acceptable substitute for consent*. It should be accepted that PSYOPs are a prerequisite component of the preparation of the mission deployment area.

All too often, intelligence, in both the gathering and analysis components, is perceived as a hostile action. A peacekeeping operation being, almost by definition, a peaceful mission, is perceived as incompatible with any intelligence effort. The inevitable implication of such a logic is that peacekeeping forces must be blind, deaf (without intelligence collection) and brainless (without intelligence analysis). If future peacekeeping operations are ever to become an endeavor meeting their goals, *intelligence activities will have to be made acceptable for all parties involved*: the countries sending peacekeeping forces, the host countries and all the warring factions. A number of arguments can be made in favor of the thesis that intelligence activities, in support of peacekeeping operations, should be acceptable to all parties:

i. If intelligence efforts are not officially undertaken by the peacekeeping force, they will rely primarily on informal or covert national or coalition resources. It is dubious whether such a situation is preferable for the parties to the conflict due to the inevitably high degree of secrecy behind the resulting decision-making processes and subsequent actions as well as to the high risk of intelligence "sanitization" and outright manipulation;

ii. All parties to a conflict have, again by definition, interests which they want to protect from intelligence efforts. In many cases such a desire is perfectly legitimate. Intelligence activities include all the activities in the broad spectrum between "spying" and "verification activities". It is in the direct interest of the warring parties to steer the peacekeeping forces' intelligence efforts away from "spying" and towards "verification activities". The major intelligence needs of a peacekeeping force should be addressable by verification-type of activities. For this reason, it is desirable for the parties to the conflict to *participate in negotiations demarcating the "legitimate" and "prohibited" intelligence missions and means*;

iii. If a peacekeeping force is prohibited from gathering its own intelligence, it becomes susceptible to manipulation and pressure by active disinformation efforts, media, staged actions, etc. Hence, it can be stated that *the parties which benefit most from an intelligence deprived peacekeeping force are those with a hidden agenda and those most interested in manipulating the peacekeeping force.*

Unless one considers a peacekeeping operation as a hostile action, the intelligence efforts in support of a peacekeeping operation should not be considered as hostile either. PSYOPs and intelligence activities in support of a peacekeeping operation should be viewed not only as acceptable, but as an essential component of any peacekeeping operation.

II. Information: Summary and Analysis of the DCR Project Questionnaires[2]

Information, the role of the media, information efforts and psychological operations have played an important role in recent peacekeeping operations. When asked whether communications and public relations efforts were of importance to their mission, the vast majority of peacekeepers answered, "yes" (79: yes; 8: no).[3] When asked to explain their answer, they replied that these efforts:

- Demonstrate our will and commitment to achieving the mission;
- Build confidence in the neutrality of the UN force;
- Help to correct the biases often present in the international media;
- Help to convince the local authorities to provide their support for the demilitarization process;
- Counter the warring parties' own psychological efforts, including local propaganda against the UN;
- Gain the confidence of the local population in our operations. This confidence is essential for maintaining the momentum of the operation;
- Keep the population informed of our goals and prevent incorrect perceptions about our presence and purposes from arising;
- Stimulate the incoming flow of information from the population;
- Gain the confidence of the members of the warring parties, particularly those lower in the chain of command;
- Help to explain to members of a faction the mutual disarmament occurring on the other side;
- Build up trust between the parties in order to assist in the exchange of prisoners of war and the bringing of humanitarian relief for refugees.

---

[2] Analysis of UNIDIR's *Practitioners' Questionnaire on Weapons Control, Disarmament, and Demobilization during Peacekeeping Operations*, Geneva, January 1995, section 3, questions 10.1-10.24, across all case studies.

[3] The reader should keep in mind that due to the nature of the *Practitioners' Questionnaire* and the manner in which it was distributed, too much importance should not be attached to any sort of statistical analysis of the data. The data obtained through the questionnaires is primarily substantive, and therefore, best suited for qualitative, rather than quantitative analysis. The reader is advised to focus - as this study does - on the substantive products of the questionnaires rather than on the occassional numerical ratio.

While the information component of peacekeeping operations was recognized by a majority of respondents, only a minority responded positively when asked whether "a well-funded and planned communication effort to support and explain their mission and activities to the local population" was undertaken (36: yes; 52: no). When asked who was in charge of briefing the general public in the mission area, the answers included:

Organized:

- the battalion HQ
- the Force HQ
- local commanders
- civil affairs
- the sector HQ
- "on our own initiative"

Carried out:

- intelligence staff officer
- civil affairs
- PSYOP units
- commanders in the field
- the battalion HQ
- the UN command
- "all units"
- "on our own initiative"

What is plainly obvious from these answers is that *when* a public information or PSYOP effort was undertaken, it was almost always "at the initiative" of different people or commands. These efforts, conducted largely by untrained personnel, were improvised, un-coordinated and were not directed towards the dissemination of a command message or in support of a common mission goal. With the exception of the efforts of certain countries participating in the peacekeeping operation (most notably the US PSYOPs), *no systematic public information effort was included in the planning of most peacekeeping operations*.

Finally, it is interesting to note that according to the UNIDIR questionnaire, when efforts were undertaken, they centered around radio or TV broadcasts and the dropping of leaflets.[4] These means can, however, be ineffective in certain regions because of the very low literacy rate or because only few people have access to radios or TV.

III. Psychological Operations and Civil Affairs

> PSYOP should be viewed as any other weapon system in a commander's arsenal - a nonlethal, yet psychological causality-producing weapon system that is an extraordinary force multiplier.
>
> Major Robert B. Adolph Jr.[5]

Efforts aimed at influencing enemy behavior are not a new phenomenon in contemporary warfare. For example, 65,000,000,000 leaflets were dropped by Allied Forces on Axis territory during the Second World War.[6] During DESERT STORM, 29,000,000 leaflets were distributed by US forces between 30 December 1990 and 28 February 1991.[7] More recently, 960,000 leaflets were dropped by US forces over Bosnia-Herzegovina during the night preceding the beginning of the PROVIDE PROMISE operation.[8] Psychological operations are not new to warfare. In fact, the Chinese strategist Sun Tsu already had stated 2,400 years ago that the best way to win a war is to get your enemy to surrender without fighting: "for to win one hundred victories in one hundred battles is not the acme of skill. To subdue the enemy without fighting is the acme of skill".[9] What is rather new, however, is the creation of special units dedicated to the actions aimed at the enemy's mind.

---

[4] *Ibid.*

[5] Major Robert B. Adolph Jr. "PSYOP: Gulf War Force Multiplier", *Army*, December 1992, p. 16.

[6] South African Defence Force Manual, *Techniques of Propaganda and Counter Propaganda*, Annex A-1.

[7] *Ibid.*, p. 18.

[8] H. Allen Holmes (Assistant Secretary of Defense for Special Operations and Low-Intensity Conflicts), and General Wayne A. Downing (Commander in Chief of the US Special Operations Command), *United States Special Operations Forces: Posture Statement*, 1994, p. 24.

[9] Sun Tzu, *The Art of War*, Oxford: Oxford University Press, 1963, p. 77.

The United States Special Operations Forces (SOF) probably represent the best known force with a dedicated PSYOP component: the US Army Special Operations Command's Civil Affairs/Psychological Operations Command in Fort Bragg, North Carolina which controls a number of PSYOP groups. Each PSYOP group consists of five active and eight reserve battalions. They can be supported by the US Air Force Special Operations Command at Hurlburt Field, Florida, which controls 4 squadrons of MC-130 COMBAT TALON aircraft which can be used for leaflet drops and with one Air National Guard Group equipped with EC-130 COMMANDO SOLO aircraft which are used for television and radio broadcasts. Other, non-specialized aircraft can be equipped with specially configured M-129E1 leaflet-dispensing bombs or powerful loudspeakers. Leaflets can also be distributed by 155-mm artillery shells.

The motto of the US PSYOPs - *Verbum Vincet/Win the Mind, Win the Day* - demonstrates the importance given by the US Armed Forces to the conduct of indirect actions aimed at supporting regular forces. This awareness stems in part from the experience of the Vietnam War during which the military defeat of the United States was greatly assisted by the US defeat in the propaganda war. Furthermore, even a party which does not possess a dedicated PSYOP capability can use the media, or even simple rumors, in a manner which can affect the outcome of combat operations in a decisive way. During the Russian military operation in Chechnya, the "Minister of Information" of Chechen separatists reportedly claimed that the he had obtained a copy of a Russian government plan signed on 1 December 1994 by Russian Prime Minister Chernomyrdin which ordered all Chechens to be deported from the Chechen Republic to other Russian regions.[10] Had this disinformation been largely circulated in the conflict area, it could have had a very strong impact on the Chechen's population. Interestingly, the Russians later admitted that "one of the fundamental failures of the operation was the poor organisation of the informational-explanatory efforts among the local population".[11]

What is true of a military operation is often also true for a peacekeeping operation. Whatever the mandate and intentions of the peacekeeping forces are, it is crucial first to explain them to the population in the mission area and, second, to counter-act hostile PSYOP activities. The peacekeeping force can be accused of being biased and supplying weapons to one party to the conflict, of intending to body-search women (which in many countries is a grave offense), of arresting

---

[10] Timothy L. Thomas, "Chechnya: The Russian Armed Forces Confront Chechnya", *Journal of Slavic Military Studies*, vol. 8, no. 2, June 1995, p. 283.

[11] *Chechenskaia Tragedia. Kto Vinovat.* Moscow: RIA Novosti, 1995, p. 86.

faction leaders, etc. Such accusations will be denied, of course, but much damage will already be done. One senior US Special Forces officer told the author that, as far as he was concerned, he would not even consider initiating an operation without a PSYOP preparation of the mission area or without PSYOP support.[12]

If the advantages of PSYOPs are such, one could wonder why peacekeeping operations are not routinely planned with an aggressive PSYOP component? Two possible explanations for this are the beliefs that 1) peacekeeping forces must remain neutral and cannot engage in propaganda and 2) that PSYOPs are a form of propaganda which use misrepresentation and lies. These concerns are not necessarily justified because, in the words of a US specialist, "PSYOP is most effective when it tells the truth",[13] because when PSYOPs mislead their target they rapidly lose in credibility. This is particularly true for a peacekeeping operation because, while deceptive PSYOPs can be very effectively used in order to trick an enemy in order to achieve surprise, a peacekeeping operation cannot be "won" in one single action. For the same reason, PSYOPs in support of a peacekeeping operation should not be approached as propaganda simply because over time, such an approach will be detrimental to the credibility of the peacekeeping forces and their mission. In a peacekeeping operation, PSYOPs can be seen as a capability which provide three services to the peacekeeping forces:

1. Information: as is frequently said, truth is often the first causality of war. An independent and accessible source of information which over time becomes credible can be very appreciated by the population of a conflict zone;

2. Explanation: PSYOPs can be used simply to explain the aims and means of a peacekeeping force. It is disturbing to see that in many peacekeeping operations far more efforts were directed at informing the press corps than at informing the local population; such an approach leaves the responsibility for informing the population to the local media. The very well known fact that the local press was often completely controlled by the warring factions did little to change this approach;

3. Dialogue: PSYOPs must not be seen as a "one-way street" in which leaflets are dropped and loudspeakers are directed at a passive population. This is particularly true for a peacekeeping operation whose outcome very often depends on the goodwill of the local population. The establishment of a

---

[12] Interview with General Richard W. Potter at UNIDIR.

[13] Adolph, "PSYOP: the Gulf War Force Multiplier", p. 16.

dialogue between the local population and the peacekeepers can also be viewed as a PSYOPs effort aimed at "inducing or reinforcing attitudes favorable to the peacekeeping operation".

A good example of such a dialogue effort can be found in the organization of call-in radio shows by the UN civil affairs in UN Sector West in Western Slavonia during the first years of the United Nations (UNPROFOR) operation. The idea for such a radio talk show came from the UN officer responsible for civil affairs in Sector West, Gerald Fisher, who realized upon his arrival that almost nobody in the Sector had heard about the Vance Plan and its modalities. Furthermore, both the Croat and Serb sides viewed UNPROFOR with hostility and suspicion. In view of these circumstances, the Sector Commander and the civil affairs official decided to organize weekly call-in radio talk shows during which they answered any questions the listeners might have. These shows, which were never recorded and were aired only "live", were centered around two weekly shows, one in the Croatian-held town of Daruvar and one in Serb-held Okucani. Each show lasted for an hour or two and typically had about ten listeners calling to ask questions; between questions, music was played.

These UN call-in talk shows had a difficult start: initially, most callers were very hostile to the UN presence and used the opportunity to accuse UNPROFOR of corruption, trafficking, bias, etc. What was particularly difficult for the UN representatives was the fact that not all such accusations were completely unfounded; nevertheless, with diplomacy and forthrightness even the more difficult questions were answered. Soon, however, the nature of the questions asked began to change. New questions included requests for practical information on many matters such as withdrawing money from bank accounts in banks under the control of the other faction, information on refugees, pleas for assistance for persecuted relatives, inquiries on the possibility to correspond with relatives, or to visit them, or to attend a funeral in "enemy territory". The UN began providing a very valuable assistance and information service to the local population on both sides while thereby achieving an important public relations success: UNPROFOR was now gradually seen by many not as an enemy or an invading force, but as a very real help. In the opinion of Gerald Fisher, impartiality and objectivity were the key to this success: both sides were getting a balanced assistance deal from UNPROFOR.

Clearly, these efforts went beyond "regular" PSYOPs. For example, a number of callers expressed the desire to travel in the enemy controlled zone while others requested the assistance of UNPROFOR to free their relatives. Such requests were answered not only on-air, but also by extensive follow-up which included escorting civilians in the enemy-controlled zones or night trips to prisons in order to free civilians before they would disappear or simply be shot.

While it is beyond the scope of this paper to examine in detail the history of UN Sector West,[14] it is stressed by many UNPROFOR personnel, which served there, that the psychological operations effort was crucial for the relative success of the UN operation in the sector, at least during its initial phase.

In the context of a peacekeeping operation, PSYOPs should not be limited to "positive" efforts, but should also include *counter-PSYOP* efforts. Indeed, due to the very political nature of peacekeeping operations, "information warfare", conducted through the media or otherwise, represents an always present danger for the peacekeeping force. It is thus essential for the peacekeepers not only to be aware of the risks posed by hostile PSYOP efforts, but also to be able to forcefully react to them. According to a Russian specialist, such counter-PSYOPs measures could include, among others, activities such as:

1. Definition and preservation of clearly defined and understandable political positions and objectives (i.e. a clarity in the mandate and goals);
2. Prompt responses to events and transmission of anticipatory information;
3. Systematic collection and analysis of information on the morale, mental attitudes, rumors, etc.;
4. Efforts aimed at unmasking hostile PSYOP efforts and creating mind sets permitting their critical perception;
5. Collection and dissemination of facts with the aim of discrediting enemy PSYOP efforts as simple propaganda;
6. Scouting and destroying hostile PSYOP subunits and equipment;
7. Predicting and preempting hostile PSYOP efforts in order to neutralize them.[15]

The key factor remains, however, the nature of the objectives of the peacekeeping mission and the actions of the forces participating in it. In other words, the best defense against hostile PSYOPs is a praise-worthy mission objective executed with competence:

---

[14] This was done in UNIDIR's DCR Project Case Study Paper, Barbara Ekwall-Uebelhart and Andrei Raevsky, *Managing Arms in Peace Processes: Croatia and Bosnia-Herzegovina*, Geneva: United Nations, 1996.

[15] Lt Col K. Ployakov, "War for Minds (Psychological Operations and Countermeasures)", *Morskoi Sbornik*, no. 4, April 1993, pp. 58-63.

> The greater the measure of justice, humanitarianism and of military and social competency in the actions of the command, the fewer possibilities the PSYOP organs of the enemy have for exploiting the real problems of our troops (forces) in his own interest.[16]

In the words of Colonel Jeffrey Jones, former commander of a US PSYOP group, "truth is our best weapon".[17] This fact should be put at the very core of the argument in favor of PSYOP activities in peacekeeping operations. While nobody disputes the fact that propaganda, lies, manipulations, deception, etc. can be used for PSYOP purposes, they usually have a limited value and can, if unveiled or poorly executed, become very counter-productive.

The Gulf War was the scene of a memorable example of sloppy PSYOP efforts when an Iraqi radio broadcast aimed at US forces suggested to them that their wives and girlfriends were at home "sleeping" with actor Tom Selleck and the television cartoon character Bart Simpson. This reduced the Iraqi PSYOPs to a laughingstock.[18] Competently designed and delivered PSYOP efforts aimed at deceiving the opposition were considered by US forces on a number of occasions and, reportedly, included morphing the image of Saddam Hussein sipping whisky and eating ham, both forbidden by Islam, or synthesizing the voice of the late Haitian dictator François "Papa Doc" Duvalier to urge superstitious soldiers to surrender to the US forces.[19] In both cases US PSYOPs commanders reportedly claimed that "ethics and strategy" argued against such tactics. Whether ethics really had anything to do with the decision to abandon such tactics is unclear. What is, however, obvious, is that such tactics would have been inevitably uncovered and that such a disclosure would have undermined the credibility of US PSYOPs for a long time.

PSYOPs in general, and PSYOPs in support of a peacekeeping operation in particular, cannot be reduced to a "con game". In the context of a peacekeeping operation, "success" can only be defined as "peace" and "peace", contrary to "victory", cannot be achieved by lies or manipulation. It is precisely for this reason that a peacekeeping force engaging in deception and manipulation will inevitably be perceived as a party to the conflict and, hence, as a combatant and a legitimate target. While some tactical advantages might result from a carefully orchestrated deception effort, the inevitable long-term negative consequences of such actions will dwarf their short-term benefits.

---

[16] *Ibid.*

[17] Douglas Waller, "Onward Cyber Soldiers", *Time*, 21 August 1995, p. 31.

[18] Adolph, "PSYOP: the Gulf War Multiplier", p. 16.

[19] Waller, "Onward Cyber Soldiers", p. 31.

In many operations, particularly peacekeeping operations, PSYOP activities are carefully coordinated with civil affairs (CA) efforts. CA specialists are tasked with responsibilities ranging from establishing a good relationship between the military and the civilian authorities in the mission area, to re-building destroyed facilities, to securing basic sanitation, re-establishing communications, etc. As such, CA must work in close cooperation with the intelligence and PSYOP staff officers and subunits of a peacekeeping force: jointly, they will establish the needs, design a response, interact with the local population and undertake measures to respond to the situation. Three examples taken from the US CA operations in Haiti after the US occupation illustrate the nature of CA missions:

1. "Operation Light Switch":
This operation aimed at restoring public lighting and restoring the water supply in Port-au-Prince. These efforts were undertaken in coordination with the UN Children's Emergency Fund (UNICEF) and the US Agency for International Development (USAID).

2. "Operation Police Call":
This operation, designed jointly between US PSYOP and CA planners aimed at improving the appearance of Haitian cities and was initiated in Port-au-Prince. USAID provided cleaning supplies while US military personnel directed 23,000 Haitian civilians in their efforts to clean their cities.

3. The "Adopt-a-School Program":
US CA proposed that individual US military units "adopt" a school and take responsibility for providing it with supplies needed to begin classes. As a result of this action 45 % of Haitian schoolchildren were able to start school on schedule.[20]

CA activities on the island also included the re-opening of Haitian gas stations, the restoration of Haitian customs in order to improve the flow of goods into the island, the re-opening of the Fort Liberté Central Market, a weapons buy-back program, etc. This was a vast and successful effort to establish good relations between the US forces and the local civilian population. In fact, US planners now view such efforts as essential to the overall success of the mission:

---

[20] Lt Col Stephen R Browers, "Restoring Normalcy: Army Civil Affairs Specialists Played a Critical Role in Haiti", *Armed Forces Journal*, March 1995, p. 18.

> We now recognize that "non-military" activities have a clear and direct military purpose.[21]

Recent experiences show that the planning of "non-military" activities must be integrated from the very beginning of the planning of any military operation, including a peacekeeping operation. These experiences also show that PSYOPs, CA and intelligence are all essential force multipliers in any military operation. However, while they are distinct in their methods and goals, they need to work together and in close coordination with the rest of the force and its staffs. According to US Rear Admiral Dennis Blair, Associate Director of Central Intelligence for Military Support, "unless you have very precise, very good intelligence information, warfare is not worth doing".[22] Unless "non-military" force multipliers are made available to peacekeeping forces, peacekeeping might turn out not to be worth doing.

Finally, it should also be remembered that even once a peacekeeping mission is successfully completed, CA and psychological operations are an essential component of nation-building and other reconstruction activities. In the words of a US specialist of international security and intelligence issues, "postconflict activities require the ability to communicate and inform; to exclude psychological operations does not make sense".[23]

IV. Intelligence: Summary and Analysis of the DCR Project Questionnaires[24]

Of all the issues addressed by UNIDIR's questionnaire, the importance of intelligence in a peacekeeping operation was the only issue on which all respondents were unanimous: when asked the question, "Do you think that normal information collection assets (i.e. intelligence) could and should be used for peacekeeping and disarming purposes?" all respondents replied positively (88:

---

[21] *Ibid.*

[22] Barbara Starr, "Interview with US Rear Admiral Dennis Blair, Associate Director of Central Intelligence for Military Support", *Jane's Defence Weekly*, 28 October 1995, p. 32.

[23] Richard H. Shultz, Jr., *In the Aftermath of War: US Support for Reconstruction and Nation-Building in Panama Following JUST CAUSE*, Maxwell Air Force Base, Alabama: Air University Press, August 1993, p. 73.

[24] Analysis of UNIDIR's *Practitioners' Questionnaire*, section 3, questions 10.1-10.24, across all case studies.

yes; 0: no).[25] In the words of Lt Col Potgieter, one of UNIDIR's military specialists tasked with the analysis of the questionnaires, "the importance of [the intelligence] capability cannot be over-emphasized" and "this is also the first line of defence against any threat and is a critical factor in determining mission success. It must be developed to its full potential during every military peace operation".[26]

The answers provided by the questionnaire respondents to the question "Was information always available and reliable?" are not unanimous. For example, for the United Nations Operation in Somalia (UNOSOM), 8 answers were negative and 3 positive; for UNPROFOR, the answers were 30 "no" and 19 "yes"; for United Nations Observer Group in Central America (ONUCA), 4 "no" and 7 "yes"; for United Nations Transitional Authority in Cambodia (UNTAC), 8 "no" and 6 "yes". Clearly, opinions were split on this matter. While the respondents were not provided with the systematic opportunity to justify or explain their answers, direct interviews were conducted with many of them and it is clear from these conversations that the main reason behind these seemingly contradictory answers is two-fold: the very different *intelligence requirements* of the respondents during their peacekeeping operation (depending on their mission, unit type, etc.); and the fact that *many intelligence efforts were organized and improvised at all levels of the peacekeeping forces simply because they were essential to the accomplishment of their tasks, hence the diverging appreciation of their effectiveness*.

While there was a degree of divergence on how intelligence efforts had been undertaken, the respondents were usually in agreement as to why such activities are important:

- Belligerent parties may perceive information-gathering as a hostile act. Intelligence operations may therefore destroy the trust that the parties may have in the peacekeeping force. However, it is reasonable to assume that the parties will purse their divergent aims by exploiting the presence of the peacekeeping force (as had indeed been the case during UNOSOM). They may also attempt to deceive it from time to time. Circumstances may place the force under direct attack. Such attacks may come from one of the parties to the agreement, or from extremist elements acting independently. This

---

[25] *Ibid.*, section 3, question 10.8.

[26] UNIDIR, "Analysis Report of Practitioners' Questionnaire on Weapons Control, Disarmament, and Demobilization during Peacekeeping Operations: Somalia", in Clement Adibe, *Managing Arms in Peace Processes: Somalia*, Geneva: United Nations, 1995, pp. 193 and 195.

poses a serious problem, but whatever the circumstances, the peacekeepers need information and must have the ability to collect it. The way in which it is collected is important, and it should, as far as possible, not create stones for the belligerent parties to throw back at the peacekeeping force;

- Threat capabilities are usually the first consideration in determining information requirements. It is difficult for a commander to make a decision when the picture is not reasonably clear;

- The intelligence community must define intelligence requirements for supporting the military commitment as early as possible. This is crucial because the re-deployment and planning phases of the operation require optimum support. Once deployed, a unit or formation should develop its requirements and information-gathering plan in conjunction with the operational plan, and submit it along the proper channels of command for approval. Intelligence support must always focus on operational planning considerations;

- To ensure the safety of assigned forces, the commander must have the capability to disseminate critical indications and warnings to all echelons quickly. A robust theater architecture must be in place to provide accurate and timely all-source information. This information must be formatted clearly and be at the disposal of the entire force;

- Mission success and the security of the force depends almost entirely on the observational skills of the personnel and leadership of the small unit. In the absence of other systems, human intelligence may be the primary source of timely information. This is also the first line of defense against any threat and is a critical factor in determining mission success. It must be developed to its full potential during every military peace operation;

- The military is not the only component that depends on timely information to execute their task. There may also be requirements for production of economic, political, sociological, medical and other information. It is therefore unthinkable that an operation can be successful without proper and shared information gathering capabilities.[27]

---

[27] *Ibid.*

In spite of the importance of a solid intelligence capability, the results of the questionnaire survey show that in the majority of peacekeeping operations *no force-level intelligence directives/policies were defined and that while information was provided to and exchanged with the battalions, no systematic intelligence policy was implemented.*

V. Intelligence

> Unofficially, of course, a number of RPVs with cameras fly every night over the country in support of the force HQ in Zagreb. But officially, blue helmets "have never and will never engage in intelligence activities" in Bosnia Herzegovina.
>
> Commander Franchet, UNPROFOR[28]

As we have already indicated, in UNIDIR's Disarmament and Conflict Resolution Project Questionnaire, to the question, "Do you think that normal information collection assets (i.e. intelligence) could and should be used for peacekeeping and disarming purposes?" all respondents replied positively (88: yes; 0: no).[29] This is probably the only issue pertaining to peacekeeping operations which generates such a unanimity among peacekeepers. Why is it then that, officially, "blue helmets have never and will never engage in intelligence activities"? Why is it that in such an *intelligence-intensive environment,* as any peacekeeping operation is, such a critical capability is officially rejected and covertly appreciated? A number of reasons can explain this contradiction. For example, intelligence activities, including their aims, means, methods, goals, capabilities, etc. are largely misunderstood outside the intelligence community. Furthermore, due to the often very secretive nature of intelligence activities, they are often viewed with suspicion as hostile or aggressive and as incompatible with the neutral stance of a peacekeeping force. This mixture of apprehension and dislike sometimes can turn into such an outright *phobia* of intelligence efforts that they become officially proscribed.

---

28 Commandant Franchet, *Casque Bleu Pour Rien - Ce que j'ai vraiment vu en Bosnie*, Paris: JC Lates, 1995, p. 27.

29 Analysis of UNIDIR's *Practitioners' Questionnaire,* section 3, question 10.8, across all case studies.

Intelligence has been, so far, largely forgotten in the debates surrounding the future of peacekeeping, particularly within the United Nations. As recently as 1994 even the Secretary-General's Report on the work of the Organization listed deficiencies in the areas of "communications, health services, supply, engineers and transportation".[30] The issue of intelligence was conspicuously *absent* from this report. There are many reasons for this, including the reluctance of member states to support the creation of a separate UN intelligence capability. Intelligence, and its control, yields tremendous power and, naturally, the most powerful members of the UN do not want to loose this power. Furthermore, the issue of intelligence-sharing is a politically very sensitive one. Currently, most of the intelligence-sharing within the contingents of a peacekeeping force is done on a bilateral level and only little intelligence is made available to the force.[31] If one could have a complete picture of who shares what intelligence with whom in the international community, a more accurate picture of alliances and antagonisms would emerge; such a picture could possibly look very different than the one somebody could get from numerous declarations of friendship, cooperation, mutual assistance and partnership. Finally, there is a definite degree of suspicion among many states that others could use intelligence capabilities in support of a peacekeeping operation to acquire intelligence not about the conflict, but about the methods and means of the other coalition partners.

Many states, particularly the most powerful ones, would strenuously object to any proposals aiming at creating a UN intelligence capability, at ensuring complete intelligence sharing among all contingents of a peacekeeping operation. It may be precisely for this reason that the smaller, less powerful states, should seriously consider this issue. The UN, as an organization, cannot be expected to reform its methods and operations without being tasked to do so by its member states.

Obviously, some national contingents did, and will, receive intelligence provided to them by their countries and their national intelligence collection means. The problem is, however, that it is the *entire force* which should benefit from such capabilities, not just certain contingents, and this has not been the case in the past. For example, according to the British American Security Information Council:

---

[30] B. Boutros-Ghali, *1994 Report of the Secretary-General on the Work of the Organization*, p. 57.

[31] General C.A. Carlo Jean (President of the *Centro Alti Studi per la Difensa*, Rome), *Il Controlle Degli Stati Sulla Partecipazione Delle Loro Forze Armate Alla Operazioni Di Pace*. Intervention made on 25 November 1995 at the *Istituto Affari Internazionali*, Rome.

> The international mediators in former Yugoslavia were not in receipt of North Atlantic Treaty Organisation (NATO) intelligence. Nevertheless, as individuals, each had informal access to national channels of information, through low level diplomatic traffic from their own national governments. Thus their level of private knowledge was quite high. UN Commanders in the field fared similarly, relying on their unofficial access to national intelligence. *Only the UN in New York was not informed at all* (emphasis added).[32]

Canadian General Mackenzie once said that UNPROFOR "had *absolutely no intelligence*" (emphasis added) and that he "hoped that General Rose now had satellite imagery and signals intelligence from the international community to do his job".[33] After the United States decided not to enforce the arms embargo against the Bosnian-Muslims and stopped sharing its intelligence on the embargo violations with its NATO allies, certain US officials were put in a truly absurd situation: according to UN and British sources, US admiral Smith, senior NATO commander in the Adriatic, while having full access to US intelligence reports, had to pretend during meetings with NATO colleagues that "he did not have this information".[34]

Even more disturbing events allegedly took place in the days which preceded the fall of Srebrenica to the Bosnian-Serb forces (5-11 July 1995). According to a recently published report, US intelligence services obtained information about the Bosnian-Serb preparations for the attack against Srebrenica several weeks before it took place. According to sources within the German military, this information was allegedly shared with the German intelligence service, the BND, but presumably not with the British and French intelligence services because Paris and London had accused the CIA of "interference in Bosnia in support of the Sarajevo government". This information was, at least officially, not passed to UNPROFOR or to the Security Council. Furthermore, the French intelligence services also intercepted a telephone conversation between two Bosnian-Serb generals in the week before the attack on Srebrenica. According to the same report, based on sources from the French intelligence services, this information

[32] Patricia Chilton, Otfried Nassauer, Dan Plesch and Jamie Patten (Whitaker), *NATO, Peacekeeping, and the United Nations*, London: British American Security Information Council, September 1994, p. 53.

[33] General Lewis Mackenzie, former UN Commander in Bosnia speaking in a BBC Radio interview on 11 February 1994, quoted in Chilton et al., *NATO, Peacekeeping and the United Nations*, pp. 51-52.

[34] De Vulliamy, "US Spells Out Ban on Intelligence Sharing With NATO", *The Observer*, 13 November 1994.

was given to General Janvier but "only in his capacity as French military officer and not in his role as supreme commander of the UN forces in the former Yugoslavia". Subsequently, UNPROFOR headquarters in Zagreb maintained that they had no indications of Bosnian-Serb forces planning an attack against Srebrenica.[35] Again, neither UNPROFOR, nor the Security Council, nor the Dutch contingent of UNPROFOR (deployed in Srebrenica) seem to have been given any warning about the impending Bosnian-Serb attack. Finally, it appears that when the local Dutch UNPROFOR commander, Ton Karremans, requested from the French and British supreme commanders in Sarajevo and Zagreb that they call in NATO close air support to stop the assault, both General Smith and General Janvier turned down the request without even passing it on to UN Secretary-General Boutros Boutros-Ghali, or his Special Envoy, Yasushi Akashi. General Janvier personally turned down five such requests. Only at noon on July 11, just hours before the city fell to the attackers, was such a request passed to Mr Akashi, who approved it and called in NATO aircraft.[36] Interestingly, NATO later demanded that the "UN civilians" be taken out of the decision-making for any future air strikes as a condition for further NATO air action in support of UNPROFOR, due to their alleged "indecision".

The issue of intelligence sharing is clearly one of the most controversial and difficult dilemmas which will have to be tackled by the United Nations or any other organization before it mandates a peacekeeping operation.[37] It should be recognized that since all contingents of a peacekeeping force are equally put at risk in the course of a peacekeeping operation, they should enjoy the same degree of protection too. Therefore it is reasonable to state that *every nation who gives its consent to the creation of a peacekeeping force and which sends a contingent in support of this force should be entitled to a full access to all the information available to its coalition partners which can influence the events in the mission area.*

The need to change Cold War era intelligence sharing practices is gradually being recognized by an increasing number of security specialists. For example,

---

[35] Andreas Zumach, "Intelligence Agencies Fail to Supply Information to War Crimes Tribunal", *BASIC Reports: Newsletter on International Security Policy*, 20 November 1995, no. 48.

[36] *Ibid.* and Andreas Zumach, "Western Policy in Bosnia", *BASIC Reports: Newsletter on International Security Policy*, 20 July 1994, no. 46.

[37] For a discussion on this problem see, Andrei Raevsky, "Peacekeeping Operations: Problems of Command and Control", *UN Peacekeeping in the 1990s*, Ramesh Thakur and Carlyle A. Thayer ed., Boulder, CO: Westview Press, August 1995.

in a recent paper of the British American Security Council reviewing the Dayton Accords, the following recommendation was included:

> NATO must change its current doctrine which forbids any intelligence sharing with non-NATO bodies or countries.[38]

If a country is not willing to commit itself to such intelligence-sharing with all its partners, it should either withdraw from the operation or, at a minimum, openly state its refusal to play by these rules which would then put the responsibility for withdrawing or remaining in the peacekeeping force upon the countries which will be excluded from forthright information sharing.[39] The issue of the intelligence-sharing mechanism should, ideally, *be decided before the decision to send peacekeepers in is made*. This does not mean that any country participating in a peacekeeping force must commit itself to sharing all the intelligence it might have with all its coalition partners; this only means that it commits itself to share all the information it gives its own contingent with all the other contingents of the Force. Clearly, certain countries will be uncomfortable with such views (which are only submitted here as a basis for discussion). It must be kept in mind, however, that if a peacekeeping operation is dependent upon capabilities which it does not directly control, it faces the risk of being "hijacked" by whomever controls these capabilities: "mission creep" and, subsequently, "*mandate* creep" will result in a completely different kind of operation and will eventually result in inevitable tensions between different coalition partners.

It is sometimes assumed that peacekeeping intelligence needs are primarily centered around such matters as identifying arms caches, locating movements of forces, keeping track of weapon movements, etc., while in fact intelligence needs can be much wider. For example, Colonel Bendini, one of the commanders of the Argentinean battalion in UN Sector West, described in an interview at UNIDIR how one morning a large number of refugees from Bosnia crossed the Sava river and entered Sector West. Neither the battalion commanders nor the Sector commander had received any advance notice of this movement; they were, however, somehow expected to provide assistance and security for the refugees. Typically, the Sector forces were already stretched in terms of manpower, logistics and tasks and no preparations had been made in preparation for such an additional

---

[38] Marin Gerskovic and Daniel Plesh, "Review of the Dayton Accords", *Basic Papers: Occasional Papers on International Security Issues*, 11 December 1995, p.2.

[39] See, for example, Richard A Serrano, "USA: Halt Secret-Sharing with U.N., GOP Urges", *Los Angeles Times*, 18 March 1995.

burden. This is precisely the type of situation which prompted the following assessment by UNIDIR's questionnaire analyst:

> The military is not the only component that depends on timely information to execute its task. There may also be requirements for production of economic, political, social, medical and other information. It is therefore unthinkable that an operation can be successful without proper and shared information-gathering capabilities.[40]

There is, of course, also a military requirement for a solid intelligence capability during a peacekeeping operation. Ideally, a vigorous intelligence effort should be viewed as a *prerequisite first action before* the decision is made to even initiate a peacekeeping operation: a responsible authority cannot simply assume that a peacekeeping operation is necessarily a "good thing". Furthermore, in the case of an operation supposedly enjoying the consensus of the warring parties, it is essential to determine first whether this support is real or only a facade and secondly, to make an estimate as to how the positions of the parties might evolve after the operation is initiated. As UNOSOM and UNPROFOR have demonstrated, relying solely on the half-hearted declarations of support of the different parties in conflict is not enough to ensure that the parties will not obstruct or oppose, sometimes violently, the actions of the peacekeeping force. Before a decision has been made to initiate a peacekeeping operation, the intelligence efforts should, at a minimum, be directed to establish the following:

1. Geography: terrain features, physical characteristics of the main axis of communications, suitable areas of deployment, available resources, key nodes and choke points, weather conditions, natural and man-made hazards, etc. Secure the availability of *suitable* maps.;
2. Parties to the conflict: leadership, outside supporters, cultural background and specificity, religion, politics, social structures, etc.;
3. Military forces: manpower, equipment holdings, table of organization and equipment of the different units, tactics, command and control, logistics and support, etc.;
4. Other armed forces: paramilitaries, foreign mercenaries, bandits, etc.;

---

[40] UNIDIR, "Analysis Report of Practitioners' Questionnaire on Weapons Control, Disarmament, and Demobilization during Peacekeeping Operations: Former Yugoslavia", in Ekwall-Uebelhart and Raevsky, *Managing Arms in Peace Processes: Croatia and Bosnia-Herzegovina*, p. 335.

5. Third parties: presence and activity of non-governmental organizations (NGOs), humanitarian organizations, regional or religious organizations, etc.;
6. Prospective entry and exit conditions for the peacekeeping force. The worst-case of a strong armed opposition should be planned for in both phases including the availability of additional forces sufficiently available for an *emergency extraction of the peacekeeping force under hostile fire.* Such contingency plans must be made *before* the peacekeeping force is sent in;
7. Finally, on the basis of this data, it should be verified whether objectives which are *clear, achievable within a limited time frame and which serve an overall strategy* can be defined. *A strong intelligence capability is the best prevention against mission-creep.*

It should be noted that these efforts should not be limited to the deployment area and should also include all adjacent areas which can *influence* the situation in the immediate deployment area. For this reason, the area of *intelligence responsibility will always be larger than the mission area* and the intelligence community tasked with supporting the peacekeeping force should be appropriately mandated to operate within the entire area of intelligence responsibility.

Once an "intelligence picture" has been established and if the decision to send a peacekeeping force has been taken, the intelligence planning should, in addition to continually updating the initial intelligence picture, be directed to focus on the following topics:

1. Establishing the intelligence requirements of the peacekeeping force, including an estimate of the likely intelligence gaps which could frustrate the action of the peacekeepers or put them at risk. An intelligence plan should be formulated and executed;
2. Definition of the intelligence component on all levels of the peacekeeping force including staff, decentralized collection arrangements, staff procedures, liaison officers, dedicated intelligence units, intelligence flow (exchange, feedback, requirements, etc.) architecture between the various intelligence agencies, forces, contingents both horizontally and vertically; such a dissemination must be *adapted, accurate and timely.* Particular attention should be given to a smooth exchange of information between the different joint and/or combined Headquarters (HQs). The creation of a joint intelligence center might be advisable;
3. All the information collected should also be centralized, updated, analyzed, and made available to the authorities (governments, UN, regional, etc.) responsible for the definition of the mandate of the peacekeeping force.

Every peacekeeping mission is different, therefore, principles must be adapted to every particular operation. This has, amazingly, not been the case in the past where even obvious intelligence requirements were not addressed (as, for example, in the case of the Italian Air Force contingent of United Nations Transitional Authority Group (UNTAG) which brought its own water from Italy to Rundu, Namibia, only to realize that Rundu is one of the places in Namibia with the most water).[41]

Another question which will have to be addressed in the future is the issue of the openness of the peacekeeping force to the scrutiny of the parties to the conflict. Although by their very nature, all intelligence activities arouse suspicions, they remain an *absolutely essential component of any peacekeeping operation*; in the past such activities were either conducted covertly, or imposed upon the warring factions, or left to the improvisational skills of the different contingents. For example, in Bosnia, British SAS units conducted covert intelligence gathering around the cities of Gorazde and Maglaj: they provided General Rose with detailed assessments of Bosnian-Muslim and Bosnian-Serb capabilities and facilitated the operations of other UN forces.[42] Such actions, while perfectly legitimate from a military point of view and not *necessarily* indicative of any hostile intent, do inevitably raise suspicions on all sides, including not only the warring parties, but even coalition partners (as seen by the numerous accusations made, anonymously, by UN and NATO officials, against the alleged US covert actions, and agenda, in Bosnia and Croatia).[43] It is, hence, imperative that all militarily essential and legitimate activities conducted in support of a peacekeeping force be "de-criminalized". For this, they need to be explained to all the parties involved and presented as "verification" activities rather than "spying".

Covert actions are, by essence, conducted without the consent of the party being subjected to it. In that sense, they can be assimilated to the use of force. Regarding the use of force, the US and British army field manuals warn that the

---

[41] Colonel T. van Niiekerk, SSO Intelligence, South African Rapid Deployment Force, written response to *UNIDIR's Intelligence and Public Information Questionnaire*.

[42] Michael Evans, "SAS Plays Pivotal Role in Gorazde Pocket", *The Times*, 12 April 1994.

[43] See, for example, "UK: US 'Has Joined War' in Bosnia", *Reuters News Service*, 16 November 1994; "Russia: Russian Intelligence Officer Says West Plotted Sarajevo Market Attack", *ITAR-TASS*, 7 September, 1995; Nicholas Doughty, "UK: Allies Believe US giving Military Aid to Bosnia", *Reuters*, 16 November 1994; George Jones and Suzanne Lowry, "Bosnia: Allies suspect US Hawks of Increasing Risk of War", *Daily Telegraph*, 2 June 1995; Thierry Charlier, "Les Moudjahidins Americains en Bosnie", *Defense 2001*, January 1995, pp. 8-10; Aleksandr Oliinik, "Khorvatskaia 'Buria' Provodilas'... Po Amerikanskim Planam", *Krasnaia Zvezda*, 9 September 1995, p.3.

use of force in a peacekeeping mission, while having short-term benefits can have dangerous consequences. They use exactly the same language:

> The long term effects of force may prove substantially different from the short term ones - a tactical success resulting from the use of force may lead to a long term strategic failure.[44]

If it is accepted that the main reason behind this reality is the fact that the use of force represents what the British call "crossing of a Rubicon" without a way back to wider peacekeeping[45] (i.e., without possibility to return to a situation of consent from the parties). It would then seem reasonable to infer from this that *"covert actions" conducted outside the peacekeeping mandate might in many cases yield a substantial tactical advantage for the peacekeeping force, but only at the risk of a larger strategic failure*. Clearly, the covert action might never be discovered, and if discovered, it is likely to appear less provocative, or hostile, than an overt use of force; nevertheless, it does represent an escalation which can lead to a long term strategic failure.

One possible approach to this problem would be the creation of a "verification and information cell" including representatives of the peacekeeping force and of all the warring parties which could be tasked with discussing the information needs of the peacekeeping force. The creation of such a cell could also be presented as an important confidence-building measure aimed at alleviating suspicions and hostility among all the parties involved. Parties which would oppose such an arrangement could be told, "If your activities are in compliance with our agreements, why would your party view our efforts at establishing their genuine nature as illegitimate?" If such intelligence gathering activities resulted the obtainment of information which would embarrass a party confronted by it, this party would have the possibility to explain its position and take appropriate measures to correct the situation before the information became public knowledge. Furthermore, in such a case, rumors would have much less credibility. Likewise, such an arrangement could become an effective means of pressure upon the parties. Clearly, to be effective such an effort would need to be carefully coordinated with the PSYOP component of the peacekeeping force. Speaking about the importance of psychological-warfare campaigns in general,

---

[44] Lt Col Charles Dobbie, *Army Field Manual "Wider Peacekeeping" (Third Draft)*, UK Doctrine and Training HQ, p. 4-4; *US Army Field Manual 100-23 (Peacekeeping),* Draft version 6, Fort Monroe, VA: HQ TRADOC, pp. 1-15; 4-2.

[45] Dobbie, *Army Field Manual "Wider Peacekeeping"*, p. 2-15.

and to their importance for peacekeeping operations in particular, General Rose said that:

> If you can tell people what is going on and what you are doing for them, what your limitations are, then you won't have this business of disappointed expectations created by propagandists. And there are a lot of propagandists in any war situation.[46]

This is also true for intelligence activities: if they are ever to be "de-criminalized", then their "targets" (i.e., the warring factions) need to be educated about their nature and about their goals. Beyond the warring parties, it is the international community at large, including the intelligence agencies themselves, which might need to be informed about new ways of looking at the intelligence business. For example, the idea of negotiating "verification and information activities" with potentially hostile forces might appear as hopelessly senseless to many in the intelligence establishment. However, it should be remembered that if the United States and the Soviet Union succeeded in negotiating a number of verification activities, albeit with great difficulty, it is surely not an impossible task elsewhere. At a minimum, such an idea should be discussed rather than simply dismissed.

Another important truth which is regularly "rediscovered" and which must be remembered is that no matter how much technologically sophisticated intelligence-related hardware is made available to a peacekeeping force, human intelligence (HUMINT) remains the best and most useful source of information for low-intensity conflicts (LIC), Operations Other Than War, and peacekeeping operations. In the words of an American intelligence specialist, during a low intensity conflict "the enemy can be many groups or many things [and] that there may be no order of battle for enemy forces".[47] Because most peacekeeping operations take place in LIC-type of conditions, this is also true for the peacekeeping intelligence environment. In fact, the US military learned this lesson from conflicts as early as the US intervention in Cuba in 1906-1909[48] and as late

---

[46] Tim Ripley, "Peacekeeping With a War Machine: Interview With General Rose", *International Defense Review*, January 1995, p.11.

[47] Captain Joseph K. Smith, "MIOAC: Preparations for the El Salvador Challenge", *Military Intelligence*, October-December 1993, p. 33.

[48] Captain John E. Della-Gustina, "Intelligence in Peace Operations: the MID in Cuba 1906-1909", *Military Intelligence*, October-December 1994, p. 22.

as the UNPROFOR operation.[49] As the analyst of the UNIDIR questionnaire wrote:

> Circumstances may place the (peacekeeping) force under direct attack. Such attacks may come from one of the parties to the agreement or from bandit elements acting independently. These attacks pose a serious problem to force security and the delivery of humanitarian aid. Whatever the circumstances, the peacekeepers need information and must have the ability to collect it.[50]

In a conventional conflict, danger comes either from clearly identified enemy forces or, all too often still, from friendly fire. Most peacekeeping operations take place in an environment which, besides the "regular" warring factions, features irregular units, armed civilians, mercenaries, foreign agents, or gangs of criminals which use the conflict to prey upon the civilian population. Under such circumstances, a peacekeeping force simply cannot "assume" that any one action or attack can be attributed to some, allegedly "hostile", faction. *A peacekeeping force acting on the basis of such non-corroborated suppositions will inevitably end up being manipulated by the other factions and, hence, will end up entering the conflict on one side.*[51] It is a fact that major Security Council decisions regarding the situation in Bosnia were made on the basis of facts which were not well established at the time these decisions were made.[52]

It is thus crucial that the peacekeeping force, and the authority mandating it, be made aware of the need for a solid HUMINT capability in support of the operation. If such a capability is not available, they should be made aware of the implications and risks this entails, particularly in what regards "mission creep" and its face-saving alter-ego "mandate creep".

Modern technology also provides a host of capabilities which can be used for intelligence purposes: satellite imagery, signal intelligence, sophisticated

---

[49] James Risen, "Experts Warn US Intelligence Help Has Limits", *Los Angeles Times*, 7 June 1995.

[50] Ekwall-Uebelhart and Raevsky, *Managing Arms in Peace Processes: Croatia and Bosnia-Herzegovina,* p.335.

[51] Analysis of UNIDIR's *Practitioners' Questionnaire*, section 3, questions 10.1-10.24, across all case studies.

[52] For a detailed discussion and chronology of several such cases, see David Binder, "Anatomy of a Massacre", *Foreign Policy*, no. 97, winter 1994-1995, pp. 70-79; Hugh McManners, "Serbs 'Not Guilty' of Massacre - Bosnia", *Sunday Times*, 1 October 1995; Thierry Charlier, "Coulisses de la Bosnie", *Defense 2001*, December 1994, p. 20; Michael Evans, "Muslim Soldiers Failed to Defend Town from Serbs", *The Times*, 14 July 1995.

reconnaissance aircraft, remotely piloted vehicles (drones) packed with sensors, computers, databases, battlefield radars, infrared and thermal imagery day and night-vision systems, etc.[53] Most of this technology is well adapted for peacekeeping missions[54] and, hopefully, most of these systems will be made available to peacekeeping forces although this has generally not been the case in the past.

VII. Concluding Remarks

> The successful execution of a peacekeeping operation should lie in the art of applying minimum force. On one hand, if a party attacks the peacekeeping force with artillery, the attack should be answered by artillery, and not with a six week high intensity combined offensive. On the other hand, it must also be ensured that you don't enter a gunfight with a knife.
>
> Colonel T. van Niiekerk[55]

Although peacekeeping operations are essentially political in nature, they constitute an exceptionally challenging military environment, possibly even more so than "regular" low-intensity conflicts. While in a regular conflict the goal sought is victory over the enemy, in a peacekeeping operation it is peace rather than victory which is sought: peacekeeping and pacification are different concepts. This essentially means that "success" can only be achieved if middle- to large-

---

[53] On the capabilities provided by these new systems see, for example: Captain James R. Wolf, US Air Forces, "Implications of Space-Based Imagery", *Military Review*, April 1994, pp. 75-85; Mark Hewish and Rupert Pengelley, "Peacekeepers and Counter-Punchers: Counter-Battery Radars Hold Their Ground", *International Defense Review*, 1/1995, pp. 46-50; Jaques Marmain "The SU-24MR - 'Moscow's Eye', *Jane's Intelligence Review*, January 1993, pp. 6-10 and K. Schwarz, "Flugzeug-Report: SU-24 Aufklärungsversion der 'Fencer'", *Flug Revue*, 11/1992, pp. 74-79; Lt. Gen. Ira C. Owens, "Army intelligence Operations In Force XXI: A Key Force Multiplier", *Army*, October 1994, pp. 145-149.

[54] Lt Col David J. Dean, USAF ed., *Low-Intensity Conflict and Modern Technology*, Maxwell Air Force Base, Alabama: Air University Press - Center for Aerospace Doctrine, Research and Education, June 1986.

[55] Colonel T. van Niiekerk, SSO Intelligence, South African Rapid Deployment Force, written response to *UNIDIR's Intelligence and Public Information Questionnaire*.

scale confrontations are avoided and not simply won (small, tactical-level, clashes, while being dangerous in their escalatory potential, are not necessarily synonymous with a failure of the objectives of the peacekeeping mission). Accordingly, while the objectives of a peacekeeping mission are more complex to achieve than the ones of a low-intensity conflict, the peacekeeping environment remains militarily at least as complex and dangerous, if only because of the inherent risk of escalation. Furthermore, besides political constraints, difficult rules of engagement, often imprecise or ill-adapted mandates, etc., most peacekeeping forces suffer from the fact that they do not dispose of the support and force multipliers available to "regular" national forces. Finally, peacekeeping forces are likely to be put together from different contingents with vastly different levels of military expertise which have no, or limited experience working together. Adding further to an already long list of difficulties, their command structures will be the result of difficult political negotiations rather than of purely military considerations (while NATO is currently developing a new doctrine for combined joint task forces[56] which could be used for NATO or Western European Union (WEU) peacekeeping and peace-enforcement operations, the UN is still far from having developed a doctrine of coalition operations).

It is unreasonable to expect that such problems might be solved by the creation of a standing "UN Army"; the means and the political will to establish such a force is simply not available. This is unlikely to change in the foreseeable future. If, however, a standing "UN Army" is not an achievable objective, the establishment of permanent specialized UN subunits, such an intelligence battalion/company or a PSYOP battalion/company should prove a more achievable objective. Short of having its own force, the UN would at least dispose of its own *force multipliers*. Besides intelligence and PSYOP subunits, other types, such as engineers or signals for example, could also be envisioned.

Clearly, this proposition is laden with many problems ranging from financial issues (who would pay for the costs), to administrative predicaments (career management), to doctrinal difficulties (table of organization and equipment, engagement doctrine, etc.), to political dilemmas (who controls and commands these subunits). Nevertheless, the development of such a capability could serve as a first step towards developing a UN Army.

Besides the creation of UN capabilities, other resources are available to the international community. The civilian space-based remote sensing market offers another interesting possibility for the United Nations, or any other force, to obtain good, militarily useful, intelligence. Four main criteria are used to measure the

---

[56] Charles L. Barry "NATO's Bold New Concept - CJTF", *JFQ*, Summer 1994, pp. 45-54.

usefulness of a remote sensor[57]: resolution, sensor type, coverage and timeliness.[58] Currently, a number of countries are marketing sophisticated remote sensing capabilities (Brazil, Canada, China, France, India, Japan, Russia, the USA and the European Space Agency) which, while not as good as the superpower's military systems, offer militarily useful resolution, sensors, coverage and timeliness. For example, Russian and French systems already offer 10-meter resolution, and in the near future, 1-meter resolution systems will be offered on the market.[59] Clearly, civilian systems are rapidly closing the gap between civilian and military systems, and they have already reached a level of sophistication where they become militarily useful. If a peacekeeping force is not given access to the military capabilities available to certain governments, it could turn to this civilian market and simply contract a number of agencies to supply it with space-based remote sensing support.

The same can be said of many other technologies with intelligence applications and, again, while the sophisticated and complex capabilities available to the major powers cannot be simply purchased on the open market, a number of *militarily useful* ones can (such as, for example, electronic intelligence systems, GPS receivers, etc.). The real problem is not so much one of availability as much as one of bureaucratic and administrative authority and control; the problem is also, again, a political one.

For what regards psychological operations, the contracting of civilian agencies by the United Nations is also a possibility which should at least be considered. The civilian market offers a host of different companies which offer all types of services ranging from commercial advertisement, to public relations, to media relations. Competent consulting firms could assist the UN in determining its needs and the optimal ways to combine the capabilities of the market to address them. The costs of such contracting might be considered as too high for an organization already going through difficult financial times. But in considering these costs, one should also evaluate the costs of mission and mandate creep, of

---

[57] Captain James R. Wolf, US Air Force, "Implications of Space-Based Observation", *Military Review*, April 1994, pp. 75-85.

[58] Note: "resolution" refers to the size an object system can distinguish (also with the useof image enhancement techniques); "sensor types" fall in two main categories: optical systems (including infrared spectrums and microwave frequencies), and radars; "coverage" refers to the parts of a globe a system can observe and to the length of time between opportunities to see a specific target - the "revisit time"; "timeliness" refers to length of time between the observation of a target by a platform and the moment when it is made available to the ultimate user.

[59] Captain James R. Wolf, US Air Force, "Implications of Space-Based Observation", *Military Review*, April 1994, pp. 75-85.

military escalation and confrontation, of combat actions or of drawn out interventions.

Lastly, it is submitted that the nature of a peacekeeping operation has a direct impact upon the intelligence and psychological operations support requirements it places upon a force. The new, the so-called "six and a half", type of peacekeeping operations are in this regard the most demanding ones. Indeed, because such mission are envisioned from the outset as somewhere in the "grey zone" between traditional peacekeeping and peace enforcement, they place the biggest possible strain on the capabilities of the peacekeeping force.

It is most difficult to convince the parties to a conflict that a force is, and intends to stay, somewhere in the middle between peace enforcement and peacekeeping; once force is used, the supposed neutrality or impartiality of a force is inevitably put under question. No matter how sophisticated and dynamic the psychological operations support for a "six and a half" -type of mission is, its credibility will gradually be eroded by the very visible use of force of the peacekeepers. Almost by definition a mission designed as a "six and a half" -type will resort to the threat, albeit and even if implicit only, of use of force. Once this "Rubicon" is crossed (to use the British expression), and this Rubicon is in reality already crossed even when the use of force is only threatened, the acceptance and consent of the warring parties is almost certain to fade, and the mission and mandate creep leads the mission goals from peacekeeping to pacification. Under such circumstances it is difficult to see by what mechanism de-escalation could occur, and while the peacekeeping force might still subdue the "hostile faction", at least for a while, the initial goal of the mission, i.e. peacekeeping, is not accomplished. Pacification, always a short-term solution, might give the appearance of success but it only delays the inevitable defeat of real peace.

This phenomenon will also be reflected in the type of psychological operation efforts required by the force: from building consensus and "favourable attitudes" (towards the peacekeeping force and, more importantly, towards peace in general), the PSYOP effort will, typically, seek to promote surrender in the face of inevitable defeat and overwhelming force. This main goal being, by definition, a short-term one, will lead to a fundamental change in the goals of the psychological warfare tasks which will negatively affect the middle- to long-term needs of nation-building and reconstruction activities.

The same can be said of intelligence requirements in support of a "six and a half -type" of operation. Because of its escalatory potential, this type of operation requires a much more complex intelligence capability which, besides providing the essential intelligence support for the peacekeeping mission proper, continuously keeps track of all activities in the area affecting the peacekeeping operation and updates the intelligence picture needed for possible combat actions and the likely resulting escalation. This is an immensely complex task which can, in reality, be effectively tackled successfully only by the large and sophisticated intelligence agencies of the major military powers. It is most unlikely that the United Nations will develop similar or equivalent capabilities in the foreseeable future and equally unlikely that the major powers would share with UN contingents the intelligence they have, particularly for a "six and a half -type" of mission. Thus, it is logical to conclude that any "six and a half -type" of peacekeeping operation will be effectively controlled by the major military powers and that the decision and capability to use force against one or several parties to the conflict will not be in the hands of the United Nations, but only in the hands of a few countries. In theory, the Security Council would, of course, have to authorize any use of force, but in reality, the nations upon which the peacekeeping force would be dependent for an eventual use of force or for intelligence support will demand, and obtain, rules of engagement and mandate (re)formulations which would not limit their freedom of action, hence, free them from any "interference" from UN officials. The chain of events preceding and following the fall of Srebrenica and Zepa to the Bosnian Serbs sets in this respect a most worrisome precedent.

If the United Nations wants to maintain control over its own peacekeeping operations, it is imperative that it engage only in the type of peacekeeping operations which are commensurate with its own capabilities. Failure to do so will always result in a "loss of sovereignty" of the United Nations over the operation in favor or one or several major military powers. Such a loss of sovereignty is always accompanied by a loss of face which is most damaging to the Organization.

It is unlikely that the major powers will press for much fundamental change in the intelligence and psychological operations in support of peacekeeping operations. Since their contingents are likely to enjoy such support and since their quasi-monopoly over such capabilities yields political power, the major powers simply do not have the incentive to push for too much reform: they will satisfy themselves with offering their capabilities in support of a peacekeeping mission, but only if they can retain a complete control over them, thereby furthering their control and influence over the operation (and, by extension, over the UN). Smaller states, however, have a much larger stake in reforming the way peacekeeping operations are being conducted. It is enough to take a look at the casualty lists of recent peacekeeping operations country by country to convince oneself that the so-called "smaller" countries do not always pay the smallest price in casualties. Furthermore, peacekeeping is likely to remain a key component of UN activities in the future and small countries cannot simply satisfy themselves with what amounts to a simple handover of the decision-making and execution of such activities to a few powerful states. A loss of sovereignty over a UN operation and a loss of face for the UN is, ultimately, a loss of face for the countries composing the United Nations. The definition of peacekeeping missions commensurate with the capabilities of the UN and the support for the creation of minimal UN capabilities for such mission should thus be viewed as an objective of national interest for all UN member states.

Biographical Note

Andrei Raevsky received his B.A. in International Relations from the School for International Service of the American University, Washington DC, with specializations in International Relations and Russia/USSR Area Studies. He received his M.A. in International Relations from the Paul Nitze School of Advanced International Relations of John Hopkins University, Washington DC, with specializations in Strategic Studies and International Economics. He was a Research Associate with the United Nations Institute for Disarmament Research (UNIDIR) and the Primary Project Researcher for the UNIDIR Project on Disarmament and Conflict Resolution. He has published two research papers at UNIDIR entitled *Development of Russian National Security Policies: Military Reform* and *Russian Approaches to Peacekeeping Operations* (with Major General N.I. Vorob'ev); articles in different journals including the *Journal of Slavic Military Studies* and *Le Trimestre du Monde;* and a chapter on the problems of command and control during peacekeeping operations in *UN Peacekeeping in the 1990s,* published by Westview Press (edited by Ramesh Thakur and Carlyle A. Thayer). He is a Swiss citizen and lives in Geneva, Switzerland.

UNIDIR publications

The publications produced by UNIDIR are intended for wide dissemination through free distribution to diplomatic missions, as well as research institutes, experts, academics and sales through the United Nations Sales Section and other outlets.

Research Reports / Rapports de recherche

La guerre des satellites: enjeux pour la communauté internationale, par Pierre Lellouche (éd.) (IFRI), 1987, 42p., publication des Nations Unies, numéro de vente: GV.F.87.0.1.

* Also available in English: ***Satellite Warfare: A Challenge for the International Community***, by Pierre Lellouche (ed.) (IFRI), 1987, 39p., United Nations publication, Sales No. GV.E.87.0.1.

The International Non-Proliferation Régime 1987, by David A.V. Fischer, 1987, 81p., United Nations publication, Sales No. GV.E.87.0.2.

La question de la vérification dans les négociations sur le désarmement aux Nations Unies, par Ellis Morris, 1987, 230p., publication des Nations Unies, numéro de vente: GV.F.87.0.4.

* Also available in English: ***The Verification Issue in United Nations Disarmament Negotiations***, by Ellis Morris, 1987, 230p., United Nations publication, Sales No. GV.E.87.0.4.

Confidence-Building Measures in Africa, by Augustine P. Mahiga and Fidelis Nji, 1987, 16p., United Nations publication, Sales No. GV.E.87.0.5.

Disarmament: Problems Related to Outer Space, UNIDIR, 1987, 190p., United Nations publication, Sales No. GV.E.87.0.7.

* Existe également en français: ***Désarmement: problèmes relatifs à l'espace extra-atmosphérique***, UNIDIR, 1987, 200p., publication des Nations Unies, numéro de vente: GV.F.87.0.7.

Interrelationship of Bilateral and Multilateral Disarmament Negotiations / Les relations entre les négociations bilatérales et multilatérales sur le désarmement, Proceedings of the Baku Conference, 2-4 June 1987 / Actes de la Conférence de Bakou, 2-4 juin 1987, 1988, 258p., United Nations publication, Sales No. GV.E/F.88.0.1, publication des Nations Unies, numéro de vente: GV.E/F.88.0.1.

Disarmament Research: Agenda for the 1990's / La recherche sur le désarmement: programme pour les années 90, Proceedings of the Sochi Conference, 22-24 March 1988 / Actes de la Conférence de Sotchi, 22-24 mars 1988, Geneva, 1988, 165p.,

United Nations publication, Sales No. GV.E./F.88.0.3, publication des Nations Unies: GV.E./F.88.0.3.

Conventional Disarmament in Europe, by André Brie (IIB), Andrzej Karkoszka (PISM), Manfred Müller (IIB), Helga Schirmeister (IIB), 1988, 66p., United Nations publication, Sales No. GV.E.88.0.6.

* Existe également en français: ***Le désarmement classique en Europe***, par André Brie (IIB), Andrzej Karkoszka (PISM), Manfred Müller (IIB), Helga Schirmeister (IIB), 1989, 90p., publication des Nations Unies, numéro de vente: GV.E.89.0.6.

Arms Transfers and Dependence, by Christian Catrina, 1988, 409p., published for UNIDIR by Taylor & Francis (New York, London).

Les forces classiques en Europe et la maîtrise des armements, par Pierre Lellouche et Jérôme Paolini (éd.) (IFRI), 1989, 88p., publication des Nations Unies, numéro de vente: GV.F.89.0.6.

* Also available in English: ***Conventional Forces and Arms Limitation in Europe***, by Pierre Lellouche and Jérôme Paolini (eds) (IFRI), 1989, 88p., United Nations publication: GV.E.89.0.6.

National Security Concepts of States: New Zealand, by Kennedy Graham, 1989, 180p., published for UNIDIR by Taylor & Francis (New York, London).

Problems and Perspectives of Conventional Disarmament in Europe, Proceedings of the Geneva Conference 23-25 January 1989, 1989, 140p., published for UNIDIR by Taylor & Francis (New York, London).

* Existe également en français: ***Désarmement classique en Europe: problèmes et perspectives***, 1990, 226p., publié pour l'UNIDIR par Masson (Paris).

The Projected Chemical Weapons Convention: A Guide to the Negotiations in the Conference on Disarmament, by Thomas Bernauer, 1990, 328p., United Nations publication, Sales No. GV.E.90.0.3.

Verification: The Soviet Stance, its Past, Present and Future, by Mikhail Kokeev and Andrei Androsov, 1990, 131p., United Nations publication, Sales No. GV.E.90.0.6.

* Existe également en français: ***Vérification: la position soviétique - Passé, présent et avenir***, 1990, 145p., publication des Nations Unies, numéro de vente: GV.F.90.0.6.

UNIDIR Repertory of Disarmament Research: 1990, by Chantal de Jonge Oudraat and Péricles Gasparini Alves (eds), 1990, 402p., United Nations publication, Sales No. GV.E.90.0.10.

Nonoffensive Defense: A Global Perspective, 1990, 194p., published for UNIDIR by Taylor & Francis (New York, London).

Aerial Reconnaissance for Verification of Arms Limitation Agreements - An Introduction, by Allan V. Banner, Keith W. Hall and Andrew J. Young, D.C.L., 1990, 166p., United Nations publication, Sales No. GV.E.90.0.11.

Africa, Disarmament and Security / Afrique, désarmement et sécurité, Proceedings of the Conference of African Research Institutes, 24-25 March 1990 / Actes de la Conférence des Instituts de recherche africains, 24-25 mars 1990, United Nations publication, Sales No. GV.E/F.91.0.1, publication des Nations Unies, numéro de vente: GV.E/F.91.0.1.

Peaceful and Non-Peaceful Uses of Space: Problems of Definition for the Prevention of an Arms Race, by Bhupendra Jasani (ed.), 1991, 179p., published for UNIDIR by Taylor & Francis (New York, London).

In Pursuit of a Nuclear Test Ban Treaty: A Guide to the Debate in the Conference on Disarmament, by Thomas Schmalberger, 1991, 132p., United Nations publication, Sales No. GV.E.91.0.4.

Confidence-Building Measures and International Security: The Political and Military Aspect - A Soviet Approach, by Igor Scherbak, 1991, 179p., United Nations publication, Sales No. GV.E.91.0.7.

Verification of Current Disarmament and Arms Limitation Agreements: Ways, Means and Practices, by Serge Sur (ed.), 1991, 396p., published for UNIDIR by Dartmouth (Aldershot).

* Existe également en français: ***La vérification des accords sur le désarmement et la limitation des armements: moyens, méthodes et pratiques***, 1991, 406p., publication des Nations Unies, numéro de vente: GV.F.91.0.9.

The United Nations, Disarmament and Security: Evolution and Prospects, by Jayantha Dhanapala (ed.), 1991, 156p., United Nations publication, Sales No. GV.E.91.0.13.

Disarmament Agreements and Negotiations: The Economic Dimension, by Serge Sur (ed.), 1991, 228p., published for UNIDIR by Dartmouth (Aldershot).

* Existe également en français: ***Dimensions économiques des négociations et accords sur le désarmement***, par Serge Sur (éd.), 1991, 211p., publication des Nations Unies, numéro de vente: GV.F.91.0.18.

Prevention of an Arms Race in Outer Space: A Guide to the Discussions in the Conference on Disarmament, by Péricles Gasparini Alves, 1991, 221p., United Nations publication, Sales No. GV.E.91.0.17.

Nuclear Issues on the Agenda of the Conference on Disarmament, by Thomas Bernauer, 1991, 108p., United Nations publication, Sales No. GV.E.91.0.16.

Economic Adjustment after the Cold War: Strategies for Conversion, by Michael Renner, 1991, 262p., published for UNIDIR by Dartmouth (Aldershot).

Verification of Disarmament or Limitation of Armaments: Instruments, Negotiations, Proposals, by Serge Sur (ed.), 1992, 267p., United Nations publication, Sales No. GV.E.92.0.10.

* Existe également en français: ***Vérification du désarmement ou de la limitation des armements: instruments, négociations, propositions***, par Serge Sur (éd.), 1994, 246p., publication des Nations Unies, numéro de vente: GV.F.92.0.10.

National Security Concepts of States: Argentina, by Julio C. Carasales, 1992, 131p., United Nations publication, Sales No. GV.E.92.0.9.

* Existe également en français: ***Conceptions et politiques de la République argentine en matière de sécurité***, par Julio C. Carasales, 1992, 136p., publication des Nations Unies, numéro de vente: GV.F.92.0.9.

National Security Concepts of States: Sri Lanka, by Vernon L. B. Mendis, 1992, 205p., United Nations publication, Sales No. GV.E.92.0.12.

Military Industrialization and Economic Development. Theory and Historical Case Studies, by Raimo Väyrynen, 1992, 121p., published for UNIDIR by Dartmouth (Aldershot).

European Security in the 1990s: Problems of South-East Europe, Proceedings of the Rhodes (Greece) Conference, 6-7 September 1991, by Chantal de Jonge Oudraat (ed.) / ***La sécurité européenne dans les années 90: Problèmes de l'Europe du Sud-Est***, Actes de la Conférence de Rhodes (Grèce), 6-7 septembre 1991, sous la direction de Chantal de Jonge Oudraat, 1992, 219p., United Nations publication, Sales No. GV.E/F.92.0.14, publication des Nations Unies, numéro de vente: GV.E/F.92.0.14.

Disarmament and Limitation of Armaments: Unilateral Measures and Policies, Proceedings of the Paris Conference, 24 January 1992, by Serge Sur (ed.), 1992, 94p., United Nations publication, Sales No. GV.E.92.0.23

* Existe également en français: ***Désarmement et limitation des armements: mesures et attitudes unilatérales***, Actes de la Conférence de Paris, 24 janvier 1992, sous la direction de Serge Sur, 1992, 103p., publication des Nations Unies, numéro de vente: GV.F.92.0.23.

Conference of Research Institutes in Asia and the Pacific, Proceedings of the Beijing (China) Conference, 23-25 March 1992, 1992, United Nations publication, Sales No. GV.E.92.0.29.

Maritime Security: The Building of Confidence, by Jozef Goldblat (ed.), 1992, 163p., United Nations publication, Sales No. GV.E.92.0.31.

Towards 1995: The Prospects for Ending the Proliferation of Nuclear Weapons, by David Fischer, 1992, 292p., published for UNIDIR by Dartmouth (Aldershot).

From Versailles to Baghdad: Post-War Armament Control of Defeated States, by Fred Tanner (ed.), 1992, 264p., United Nations publication, Sales No. GV.E.92.0.26.

Security of Third World Countries, by Jasjit Singh and Thomas Bernauer (eds), 1993, 168p., published for UNIDIR by Dartmouth (Aldershot).

Regional Approaches to Disarmament, Security and Stability, by Jayantha Dhanapala (ed.), 1993, 282p., published for UNIDIR by Dartmouth (Aldershot).

Economic Aspects of Disarmament: Disarmament as an Investment Process, by Keith Hartley, 1993, 91p., United Nations publication, Sales No. GV.E.93.0.3.

* Existe également en français: ***Aspects économiques du désarmement: le désarmement en tant qu'investissement***, par Keith Hartley, 1993, 104p., publication des Nations Unies, numéro de vente: GV.F.93.0.3.

Nonmilitary Aspects of Security - A Systems Approach, by Dietrich Fischer, 1993, 222p., published for UNIDIR by Dartmouth (Aldershot).

Conference of Latin American and Caribbean Research Institutes, Proceedings of the São Paulo Conference, 2-3 December 1991, by Péricles Gasparini Alves (ed.), 1993, 202p., United Nations publication, Sales No. GV.E.93.0.8.

The Chemistry of Regime Formation: Explaining International Cooperation for a Comprehensive Ban on Chemical Weapons, by Thomas Bernauer, 1993, 480p., published for UNIDIR by Dartmouth (Aldershot).

Civil Space Systems: Implications for International Security, by Stephen Doyle, 1994, 271p., published for UNIDIR by Dartmouth (Aldershot).

Nuclear Deterrence: Problems and Perspectives in the 1990's, by Serge Sur (ed.), 1993, 173p., United Nations publication, Sales No. GV.E.93.0.16.

Conference of Research Institutes in the Middle East, Proceedings of the Cairo Conference, 18-19 April 1993, by Chantal de Jonge Oudraat (ed.), 1994, 132p., United Nations publication, Sales No. GV.E.94.0.13.

Disarmament and Arms Limitation Obligations: Problems of Compliance and Enforcement, by Serge Sur (ed.), 1994, 296p., published for UNIDIR by Dartmouth (Aldershot)

* Existe également en français: ***Obligations en matière de désarmement et de limitation des armements: problèmes de respect et mesures d'imposition***, sous la direction de Serge Sur, 1995, 430p., publication des Nations Unies, numéro de vente: GV.F.95.0.27.

European Security in the 1990s: Challenges and Perspectives, by Victor-Yves Ghebali and Brigitte Sauerwein, Avant Propos by Serge Sur, 1995, 230p., United Nations publication, Sales No. GV.E.94.0.28.

Arms and Technology Transfers: Security and Economic Considerations Among Importing and Exporting States, Proceedings of the Geneva (Switzerland) Conference, 14-15 February 1994, by Sverre Lodgaard and Robert L. Pfaltzgraff (eds), 1995, 287p., United Nations publication, Sales No. GV.E.95.0.10.

Nuclear Policies in Northeast Asia, Proceedings of the Seoul (South Korea) Conference, 25-27 May 1994, by Andrew Mack (ed.), 1995, 263p., United Nations publication, Sales No. GV.E.95.0.8.

Building Confidence in Outer Space Activities: CSBMs and Earth-to-Space Monitoring, by Péricles Gasparini Alves (ed.), 1995, 357p., published for UNIDIR by Dartmouth (Aldershot)

Disarmament and Conflict Resolution Project - Managing Arms in Peace Processes: Somalia, by Clement Adibe, 1995, 242p., United Nations publication, Sales No. GV.E.95.0.20.

Disarmament and Conflict Resolution Project - Managing Arms in Peace Processes: Rhodesia/Zimbabwe, by Jeremy Ginifer, 1995, 127p., United Nations publication, Sales No. GV.E.95.0.28.

Disarmament and Conflict Resolution Project - Managing Arms in Peace Processes: Croatia and Bosnia-Herzegovina, by Barbara Ekwall-Uebelhart and Andrei Raevsky, 1996, 411p., United Nations publication, Sales No. GV.E.96.0.6.

Disarmament and Conflict Resolution Project - Managing Arms in Peace Processes: Cambodia, by Jianwei Wang, 1996, 243p., United Nations publication, Sales No. GV.E.96.0.14.

Disarmament and Conflict Resolution Project - Small Arms Management and Peacekeeping in Southern Africa, by Christopher Smith, Peter Batchelor and Jakkie Potgieter, 1996, 125p., United Nations publication, Sales No. GV.E.96.0.16.

Disarmament and Conflict Resolution Project - Managing Arms in Peace Processes: Mozambique, by Eric Berman, 1996, 103p., United Nations publication, Sales No. GV.E.96.0.18.

A Zone Free of Weapons of Mass Destruction in the Middle East, by Jan Prawitz and James F. Leonard, 1996, 134p., United Nations publication, Sales No. GV.E.96.0.19.

Disarmament and Conflict Resolution Project - Managing Arms in Peace Processes: Liberia, by Clement Adibe, 1996, United Nations publication **(forthcoming)**

Disarmament and Conflict Resolution Project - Managing Arms in Peace Processes: Nicaragua and El Salvador, by Paulo Wrobel, 1996, United Nations publication **(forthcoming)**

Disarmament and Conflict Resolution Project - Managing Arms in Peace Processes: Haiti, by Marcos Mendiburu, 1996, United Nations publication **(forthcoming)**

Disarmament and Conflict Resolution Project - Managing Arms in Peace Processes: The Issues, by Estanislao Angel Zawels, Stephen John Stedman, Donald C.F. Daniel, David Cox, Jane Boulden, Fred Tanner, Jakkie Potgieter and Virginia Gamba, 1996, United Nations publication **(forthcoming)**

Research Papers / Travaux de recherche

No. 1 - ***Une approche juridique de la vérification en matière de désarmement ou de limitation des armements***, par Serge Sur, septembre 1988, 70p., publication des Nations Unies, numéro de vente: GV.F.88.0.5.
* Also available in English: ***A Legal Approach to Verification in Disarmament or Arms Limitation***, 1988, 72p., United Nations publication, Sales No. GV.E.88.0.5.

No. 2 - ***Problèmes de vérification du Traité de Washington du 8 décembre 1987 sur l'élimination des missiles à portée intermédiaire***, par Serge Sur, octobre 1988, 64p., publication des Nations Unies, numéro de vente: GV.F.88.0.7.
* Also available in English: ***Verification Problems of the Washington Treaty on the Elimination of Intermediate-Range Missiles***, by Serge Sur, October 1988, 62p., United Nations publication, Sales No. GV.E.88.0.7.

No. 3 - ***Mesures de confiance de la CSCE: documents et commentaires***, par Victor-Yves Ghebali, mars 1989, 112p., publication des Nations Unies, numéro de vente: GV.F.89.0.5.
* Also available in English: ***Confidence-Building Measures within the CSCE Process: Paragraph-by-Paragraph Analysis of the Helsinki and Stockholm Régimes***, by Victor-Yves Ghebali, March 1989, 110p., United Nations publication, Sales No. GV.E.89.0.5.

No. 4 - ***The Prevention of the Geographical Proliferation of Nuclear Weapons: Nuclear-Free Zones and Zones of Peace in the Southern Hemisphere***, by Edmundo Fujita, April 1989, 52p., United Nations publication, Sales No. GV.E. 89.0.8.
* Existe également en français: ***La prévention de la prolifération géographique des armes nucléaires: zones exemptes d'armes nucléaires et zones de paix dans l'hémisphère Sud***, par Edmundo Fujita, avril 1989, 61p., publication des Nations Unies, numéro de vente: GV.F.89.0.8.

No. 5 - ***The Future Chemical Weapons Convention and its Organization: The Executive Council***, by Thomas Bernauer, May 1989, 34p., United Nations publication, Sales No. GV.E.89.0.7.
* Existe également en français: ***La future convention sur les armes chimiques et son organisation: le Conseil exécutif***, par Thomas Bernauer, mai 1989, 42p., publication des Nations Unies, numéro de vente: GV.F.89.0.7.

No. 6 - ***Bibliographical Survey of Secondary Literature on Military Expenditures***, November 1989, 39p. United Nations publication, Sales No. GV.E.89.0.14.

No. 7 - ***Science and Technology: Between Civilian and Military Research and Development - Armaments and development at variance***, by Marek Thee, November 1990, 23p., United Nations publication, Sales No. GV.E.90.0.14.

No. 8 - ***Esquisse pour un nouveau paysage européen***, par Eric Remacle, octobre 1990, 178p., publication des Nations Unies, numéro de vente: GV.F.91.0.2.

No. 9 - ***The Third Review of the Biological Weapons Convention: Issues and Proposals***, by Jozef Goldblat and Thomas Bernauer, April 1991, 78p., United Nations publication, Sales No. GV.E.91.0.5.

No. 10 - ***Disarmament, Environment, and Development and their Relevance to the Least Developed Countries***, by Arthur H. Westing, October 1991, 108p., United Nations publication, Sales No. GV.E.91.0.19.

No. 11 - ***The Implications of IAEA Inspections under Security Council Resolution 687***, by Eric Chauvistré, February 1992, 72p., United Nations publication, Sales No. GV.E.92.0.6.

No. 12 - ***La Résolution 687 (3 avril 1991) du Conseil de sécurité dans l'affaire du Golfe: problèmes de rétablissement et de garantie de la paix***, par Serge Sur, 1992, 65p., publication des Nations Unies, numéro de vente: GV.F.92.0.8.

* Also available in English: ***Security Council Resolution 687 of 3 April 1991 in the Gulf Affair: Problems of Restoring and Safeguarding Peace***, by Serge Sur, 1992, 65p., United Nations publication, Sales No. GV.E.92.0.8.

No. 13 - ***The Non-Proliferation Treaty: How to Remove the Residual Threats***, by Jozef Goldblat, 1992, 36p., United Nations publication, Sales No. GV.E.92.0.25.

* Existe également en français: ***Le Traité sur la non-prolifération: comment parer les menaces***, par Jozef Goldblat, 1993, 40p., publication des Nations Unies, numéro de vente: GV.F.92.0.25.

No. 14 - ***Ukraine's Non-Nuclear Option***, by Victor Batiouk, 1992, 34p., United Nations publication, Sales No. GV.E.92.0.28.

No. 15 - ***Access to Outer Space Technologies: Implications for International Security***, by Péricles Gasparini Alves, 1992, 160p., United Nations publication, Sales No. GV.E.92.0.30.

No. 16 - ***Regional Security and Confidence-Building Processes: The Case of Southern Africa in the 1990s***, by Solomon M. Nkiwane, 1993, United Nations publication, Sales No. GV.E.93.0.6.

No. 17 - ***Technical Problems in the Verification of a Ban on Space Weapons***, by Stanislav Rodionov, 1993, 104p., United Nations publication, Sales No. GV.E.93.0.12.

No. 18 - ***Index to the Chemical Weapons Convention***, by A. Walter Dorn, 1993, 59p., United Nations publication, Sales No. GV.E.93.0.13.

No. 19 - ***Migration and Population Change in Europe***, by John Salt, 1993, 86p., United Nations publication, Sales No. GV.E.93.0.14.

No. 20 - ***La sécurité européenne dans les années 90, défis et perspectives. La dimension écologique***, par Jean-Daniel Clavel, 1993, 40p., publication des Nations Unies, numéro de vente: GV.F.93.0.15.

No. 21 - ***Les minorités nationales et le défi de la sécurité en Europe***, par Dominique Rosenberg, 1993, 45p., publication des Nations Unies, numéro de vente: GV.F.93.0.21.

No. 22 - ***Crisis in the Balkans***, by Ali L. Karaosmanoglu, 1993, 22p., United Nations publication, Sales No. GV.E.93.0.22.

No. 23 - ***La transition vers l'économie de marché des pays "ex de l'Est"***, par Louis Pilandon, 1994, 90p., publication des Nations Unies, numéro de vente: GV.F.94.0.3.

No. 24 - ***Le désarmement et la conversion de l'industrie militaire en Russie***, par Sonia Ben Ouagrham, 1993, 110p., publication des Nations Unies, numéro de vente: GV.F.94.0.4.

No. 25 - ***Development of Russian National Security Policies: Military Reform***, by Andrei Raevsky, 1994, 48p., United Nations publication, Sales No. GV.E.94.0.5.

No. 26 - ***National Security and Defence Policy of the Lithuanian State***, by Gintaras Tamulaitis, 1994, 66p., United Nations publication, Sales No. GV.E.94.0.11.

No. 27 - ***Le défi de la sécurité régionale en Afrique après la guerre froide: vers la diplomatie préventive et la sécurité collective***, par Anatole N. Ayissi, 1994, 138p., publication des Nations Unies, numéro de vente: GV.F.94.0.17.

No. 28 - ***Russian Approaches to Peacekeeping Operations***, by A. Raevsky and I.N. Vorob'ev, 1994, 182p., United Nations publication, Sales No. GV.E.94.0.18.

No. 29 - ***Une approche coopérative de la non-prolifération nucléaire: l'exemple de l'Argentine et du Brésil***, par Thierry Riga, 1994, 100p., publication des Nations Unies, numéro de vente: GV.F.94.0.22.

No. 30 - ***The CTBT and Beyond***, by Herbert F. York, 1994, 21p., United Nations publication, Sales No. GV.E.94.0.27.

No. 31 - ***Halting the Production of Fissile Material for Nuclear Weapons***, by Thérèse Delpech, Lewis A. Dunn, David Fischer and Rakesh Sood, 1994, 70p., United Nations publication, Sales No. GV.E.94.0.29.

No. 32 - ***Verification of a Comprehensive Test Ban Treaty from Space - A Preliminary Study***, by Bhupendra Jasani, 1994, 58p., United Nations publication, Sales No. GV.E.94.0.30.

No. 33 - ***Nuclear Disarmament and Non-Proliferation in Northeast Asia***, by Yong-Sup Han, 1995, 83p., United Nations publication, Sales No. GV.E.95.0.3.

No. 34 - ***Small Arms and Intra-State Conflicts***, by Swadesh Rana, 1995, 52p., United Nations publication, Sales No. GV.E.95.0.7.

No. 35 - ***The Missing Link? Nuclear Proliferation and the International Mobility of Russian Nuclear Experts***, by Dorothy S. Zinberg, 1995, 45p., United Nations publication, Sales No. GV.E.95.0.18.

No. 36 - ***Guardian Soldier: On the Future Role and Use of Armed Forces***, by Gustav Däniker, 1995, 141p., United Nations publication, Sales No. GV.E.95.0.19.

No. 37 - ***National Threat Perceptions in the Middle East***, by James Leonard, Shmuel Limone, Abdel Monem Said Aly, Yezid Sayigh, the Center for Strategic Studies (University of Jordan), Abdulhay Sayed and Saleh Al-Mani, 1995, 109p., United Nations publication, Sales No. GV.E.95.0.24.

UNIDIR Newsletter / Lettre de l'UNIDIR
(quarterly / trimestrielle)

Vol. 1, No. 1, March/Mars 1988, ***Disarmament-Development/Désarmement-Développement***, 16p.

No. 2, June/Juin 1988, ***Research in Africa/La recherche en Afrique***, 28p.

No. 3, September/Septembre 1988, ***Conventional Armaments Limitation and CBMs in Europe/Limitation des armements classiques et mesures de confiance en Europe***, 32p.

No. 4, December/Décembre 1988, ***Research in Asia and the Pacific/La recherche en Asie et dans le Pacifique***, 40p.

Vol. 2, No. 1, March/Mars 1989, ***Chemical Weapons: Research Projects and Publications/Armes chimiques: projets de recherche et publications***, 24p.

No. 2, June/Juin 1989, ***Research in Latin America and the Caribbean/La recherche en Amérique latine et dans les Caraïbes***, 32p.

No. 3, September/Septembre 1989, ***Outer Space/L'espace extra-atmosphérique***, 32p.

No. 4, December/Décembre 1989, ***Research in Eastern Europe/La recherche en Europe de l'Est***, 48p.

Vol. 3, No. 1, March/Mars 1990, ***Verification of Disarmament Agreements/La vérification des accords sur le désarmement***, 48p.

No. 2, June/Juin 1990, ***Research in North America/La recherche en Amérique du Nord***, 72p.

No. 3, September/Septembre 1990, ***Nuclear Non-Proliferation/La non-prolifération nucléaire***, 43p.

No. 4, December/Décembre 1990, ***Research in Western and Northern Europe (I)/ La recherche en Europe de l'Ouest et en Europe du Nord (I)***, 72p.

Vol. 4, No. 1, March/Mars 1991, ***Research in Western and Northern Europe (II)/La recherche en Europe de l'Ouest et en Europe du Nord (II)***, 72p.

No. 2, June/Juin 1991, ***Biological Weapons/Armes biologiques***, 40p.

No. 3, September/Septembre 1991, ***Naval and Maritime Issues/Questions navales et maritimes***, 54p.

No. 4, December/Décembre 1991, ***Bilateral (US-USSR) Agreements and Negotiations/Accords et négociations bilatéraux (EU-URSS)***, 52p.

Vol. 5, No. 1, April/Avril 1992, ***Conference on Disarmament/La Conférence du désarmement***, 63p.

No. 18, June/Juin 1992, ***Disarmament - Environment - Security/Désarmement - Environnement - Sécurité***, 52p.

No. 19, September/Septembre 1992, ***Economic Aspects of Disarmament/Aspects économiques du désarmement***, 66p.

No. 20, December/Décembre 1992, ***The Chemical Weapons Convention/La Convention sur les armes chimiques***, 100p.

Vol. 6, No. 21, March/Mars 1993, ***Research in the Middle East/La recherche au Moyen et Proche Orient***, 70p.

No. 22-23, June-September/Juin-septembre 1993, ***START and Nuclear Disarmament: Problems of Implementation/START et le désarmement nucléaire: problèmes d'exécution***, 101p.

No. 24, December/Décembre 1993, ***Peace-Keeping, Peace-Making and Peace Enforcement/Maintien, construction et imposition de la paix***, 88p.

Vol. 7, No. 25, March-April/Mars-avril 1994, ***Research in Eastern Europe and in the Newly Independent States/Recherche en Europe de l'Est et dans les nouveaux Etats indépendants***, 70p.

No. 26/27, June-September/Juin-septembre 1994, ***Non-Proliferation/Non-prolifération***, 91p.

Vol. 8, No. 28/29, December 1994-May 1995/Décembre 1994-mai 1995, ***Land Mines and the CCW Review Conference/Les mines terrestres et la Conférence d'examen de la Convention sur certaines armes classiques***

No. 30/95, June 1995-September 1995, ***Information Technology and International Security***

No. 31/95, October 1995-December 1995, ***Nuclear Disarmament: What is Next?***

How to Obtain UNIDIR Publications

1. *UNIDIR publications followed by a United Nations Sales Number (GV.E... or GV.F...) can be obtained from UNIDIR or from bookstores and distributors throughout the world. Consult your bookstore or write to United Nations, Sales Section, Palais des Nations, CH-1211 Geneva 10, Switzerland, Phone (41.22) 917.26.12, Fax (41.22) 740.09.31, or United Nations, Sales Section, UN Headquarters, New York, New York 10017, USA. The UNIDIR Newsletter is available at a voluntary subscription price of US $ 25 a year.*
2. *UNIDIR publications published by Dartmouth can be obtained through Dartmouth Publishing Company Limited, Gower House, Croft Road, Aldershot, Hampshire, GU11 3HR, England, Phone (01252) 33.15.51, Fax (01252) 34.44.05.*
3. *UNIDIR publications published by Taylor and Francis can be obtained through Taylor and Francis Ltd, Rankine Road, Basingstoke, Hants RG24 8PR, England, Phone (01256) 84.03.66, Fax (01256) 47.94.38.*